YOUR PERSONAL DESTINY:
A Complete Guide

EVANGELIST JOHN DYE

Order this book online at www.trafford.com
or email orders@trafford.com

Most Trafford titles are also available at major online book retailers.

Printed in the United States of America.

ISBN: 978-1-4669-6947-6 (sc)
ISBN: 978-1-4669-6949-0 (hc)
ISBN: 978-1-4669-6948-3 (e)

Library of Congress Control Number: 2012921910

Trafford rev. 11/20/2012

www.trafford.com

North America & international
toll-free: 1 888 232 4444 (USA & Canada)
phone: 250 383 6864 • fax: 812 355 4082

YOUR PERSONAL DESTINY:
A Complete Guide

"TABLE OF CONTENTS"

"TABLE OF CONTENTS"

YOUR PERSONAL DESTINY:
A Complete Guide

"TABLE OF CONTENTS"

"TABLE OF CONTENTS"

"TABLE OF CONTENTS"

"TABLE OF CONTENTS"

"TABLE OF CONTENTS"

"INTRODUCTION 1"

This book is dedicated to the individual walking with God, being led by the spirit in accordance with the Way, Truth and Life. (**Ultimately that's what it's about, walking with God in Love**)

When you leave this world, you will stand before God and give an account for how you lived your life.

To see, if you loved God at the end of your life & if you tried to love the people he made. (His creation)

Because it says; "he who endures to the end the same shall be saved"

God bless the reader of this book!

By Author

Evangelist John Dye

(Man of God)

"THE TRUTH"

We begin knowing, God has a big job to do and he is not willing that any should perish, but all should come to have everlasting life.

God super naturally intervenes in an individual's life to save him or her from destruction (even self destruction) to reveal the truth to them. So they will understand that God ways are higher than their ways and the ways of the world.

When God reveals this truth to you, he expects you to choose good over evil & right over wrong. He gives you a free choice to make and it's that choice that determines where you spend eternity.

God's job is to make sure that (in the end) you won't be able to say; "God didn't love me or didn't care about me and he didn't reveal the truth to me."

That would be a lie, unmistakable & undeniable because God is not willing that any should perish and he wants all to share in everlasting life, **but the choice was yours!**

Now there are consequences good or bad, depending on your choice!

"THE BEGINNING"

The individual will be allowed to come into this World by God (Gods World) and he or she will be placed with parents in which God has given a command.

Raise the child in the ways of the Lord, hoping that in the tough times the child would return to God because it has been trained in good over evil and right over wrong.

The child will leave the parents home after much time and reasoning with the parents about the word & will of God **before stepping out into this World.**

The child will be tested by the world. (Satan is allowed to test the individual)

We hope the individual has on the full armor of God & word of God, while experiencing life because people have been tempted in this World. (Even Jesus was tempted in this world)

"THE BEGINNING"

We hope the child will understand that God is in control, it's his World and he knows everything going on. (Ultimately God will make away for you to escape) He has not put more on you than you can bear and no temptation has seized you that are not common to mankind. God already knows and he has prepared the way for you to escape from it. (Sin) So you might walk in the Glory of God again!

(Sin is something or someone that takes you away from praising & believing in God)

"UN-GODLY PARENTS"

We know there are parents who do not raise their children in the Lord.

God's job is to still care for the child because the child is innocent in his sight and the child must be made aware of Gods will on Earth.

So whether the parents do it or not, God will surround that child with people supernaturally intervening in & out of the child's life to make sure the child is aware there's a God in heaven that loves him or her.

Also to make the child aware there's a book called the Bible with testimonies of people who knew God, who had encounters with God and they tried to warn others to keep their relationship with God intact.

"UN-GODLY PARENTS"

As the child is being examined by the world & he or she is making choices (We know that things unexpectedly happen to people, good & bad as was written in the book of Ecclesiastics) Solomon warned people not to let hard times, bad times, frustrations or disappointments overwhelm them. He wanted you to know that these are the times, you turn to the Lord because everyone who calls on God; we'll be saved. It is the difference between the individual that seeks to understand and know God or the individual that chooses to walk away from God for fear of knowing!

It's the difference between the advice someone accepts, the advice of God which is the way, truth and life

Or

The advice of the World that one lives in; filled with friends, family, co-workers, religions, corporations and your own desires based on the things you idolize or worship. (If one listens to this advice)

It will determine how much grief you will have in this World.

"THE WAY OF THE TRANSGR

Scripture says: "The way of the transgressor is hard"

People will begin living hard lives when they start making choices that don't include prayer to God first. They will start falling into pit holes; find themselves in bad situations with stumbling blocks in their path. They will stumble & fall and they will make multitudes of people fall with them; only then will they realize, their lives are intertwined with other people. They are causing others around them to fall & Fail. (The very thing God was trying to warn them about)

That your life is not your own, you were bought with a price! (You need an inner connection with God)

You were allowed to come here and be tested to see, if there was something in this World that could separate you from the love of God.

Oh God loves you and promised to never leave or forsake you, **but God won't make you serve him**.

You have a choice!

"THE WAY OF THE TRANSGRESSOR"

Even when you fall away, God will still come periodically and show up from time to time throughout the course of your life. Hoping you understand the Devine moments that are trying to tell you; Spiritual Law is above Physical Law or manmade law.

Breaking mans rules are one thing, but breaking Gods rules are another thing. Example: **God can save you from man, but man can't save you from God. Ultimately you must answer to God!**

"THE MESSENGERS JOB"

My job as the man of God is to make you aware of this fact and lead you to the glory of God!

So God can lead you to a blessing and bring you home in glory.

That's the messenger's job.

He's loyal & dedicated to God almighty and no other!

My mission is to improve the lives of people in this world, so they will love God & each other by motivating them to change from the pessimism of the world to optimism found in God for their own good. The results will be changes made in their Thinking & Life Style! (Making good changes bring Success & Contentment)

"RELIGION"

There are lesser forms of Godliness on Earth in this World, called religions.

They deny the power and ability of God to change people then set up manmade institutions designed to control the people. They lead multitudes of people to their own pleasures & desires for the idol worship of money, houses, cars, power, position or titles until they ultimately destroy themselves.

(Self destruction & self corruption)

Until they no longer have a relationship with God and they are left behind.

Then when they stand before God, they will be placed somewhere else because they glorified themselves and they took Gods glory to corrupt, ruin & destroy multitudes of people.

That God loved and created.

"RELIGION"

God said: "if you turn one of these little children away from me, it would be better if you were not born, a mill stone tied around your neck and cast into the sea" Because God loves the little children of the world, he does not want anyone deceiving them, tricking them and making their lives/a life of suffering for years to come. Where their mental, emotional state & heart is so distorted that it makes Gods job become harder to save them from the manipulation of the World around them.

Then God has to do everything to convert the individual soul back to understand the path of love, joy, peace, patience, kindness, goodness, faithfulness, righteousness and self control to the glory of God!

"FOR GOD OR AGAINST GOD"

Either you're for God or against God, **there is no middle ground**.

Sooner or later, you're on God side or the World side, that's why scriptures say: "do not love the World or anything in the World or anything of the World or the love of the father is not in you"

An individual who loves the World does not love God because God knows there are things that will corrupt the thinking, actions and hearts of people/ultimately making them hate God.

The individual will never have enough. (**The scriptures say, the greedy man never has enough**)

He or she will always want more & more money, houses, cars, sex, friends and parties because he or she is never satisfied or content.

But the spirit of the Lord is contentment with great peace & grace, being thankful to humbly except the salvation given by God because you know in your heart; God knows more than you and his ways are higher than your ways.

So many bow their knees in prayer saying: "holy, holy, holy is the Lord God Almighty"

"THROUGH THE STORM"

Individuals that understand, begin Praising & Thanking God for all the times, he saved them from destruction; even self destruction. (Even when they made bad decisions) They looked at their lives then recognize God was trying to warn them when he did not allow them to have things that would have destroyed them. (Even though they asked for it repeatedly) Later on in life, they looked back and knew God saved them from some of their own choices then thanked God for not allowing them to have it; people, places or things!

The scriptures say: **Man judges the outward appearance, but God judges the heart and intent of the heart to do good or evil.**

God knows the heart because he created the people, he expects them not to judge God, but to love him and move forward then call on him in time of need as you live in this world.

We walk by faith not by sight, now you're starting to grow up and build a life for yourself in this World, but trials & tribulations, ups & downs, struggles and deep rooted sins; start to ensnare the individual & lead to sickness or hospitalization, jail or prison, and frustrations; emotionally & mentally with life, but God can deliver you from these problems!

"THROUGH THE STORM"

People feel doomed in this world, **but at just the right moment & just the right time; we see how wide, how deep & how far, Gods love stretches out for the individual.** God supernaturally intervenes in the life of the individual. It's at that very moment the person can hear God and knows it's a Devine moment; not a moment someone can explain to you, not a religious moment where you go through the motions of going to church & listening to messages, listening to the preacher, trying to follow all the rules & regulations of the organization, walking by site—watching the clothes people wear; like suits & ties and doing things just the way everybody else is doing them in the congregation. And you still have problems!

It's not a matter of going to work every day & doing all that society tells you to do or trying to do things with your money & following that crowd then you still have problems. It's not a matter of going out partying or ripping & running the streets, blowing your money on drugs and alcohol; like the prodigal son and you're still in trouble. It's not a matter of listening to mom & Dad then going along with everything they say when everything they say is not the same as God and you find yourself in trouble.

"THROUGH THE STORM"

It's a **Spiritual moment**, an awakening of your soul because God has placed something in you before you ever came into the world. God placed his spirit inside of you, as a little seed then sooner or later something happens super naturally that makes it grow and open up or blossom & bloom to awaken your heart, mind, emotions and spirit **then you realize God is trying to communicate with you.**

God is trying to tell you to separate yourself from the crowd. (Step away from the crowd) Now you find yourself in a situation where momma can't help you, now you're in a situation where daddy can't help you, now you're in a situation where the preacher can't help you, now you're in a situation where friends can't help you, now you're in a situation where a husband or wife can't help you, now you're in a situation where a boy or girl friend can't help you, **now you've put yourself in a situation where there's only one who can help you and that's the Lord God almighty**! God is the only one with the answers to your problems and only he can show you the way out because he knows all things.

"THROUGH THE STORM"

It's at this moment, that you've got to be the type of person who turns to the Lord by faith and except the message; God is telling you in your heart to walk away from the crowds & groups that manipulate you and do what's best for you because God is telling you for your own good. (Individually)

If you're an alcoholic and everybody you know drinks, God is telling you/it's time to stop drinking because if you don't stop drinking; you're going to leave the world in that state. If you're a drug addict and everybody around you is doing drugs, I don't care what everybody else is doing; it's time for you to stop and turn away before you leave this world in that state. If you're a swindler & you steal money and everybody around you is a thief & kleptomaniac from corporations down to Main Street such as a street thug then God is telling you to stop stealing money from banks & corporations, stop hustling & stealing money from people in your neighborhood, stop snatching purse's and stop robbing people.

God is talking to you and he doesn't want you to leave this world in that state.

"THROUGH THE STORM"

If you're a habitual liar & trickster and you deceive everybody you know; from the pulpit & I don't care what your denomination is Baptist, Pentecostal, Methodist, Catholic, Muslim or any other name/all the way down to a Street Hustler, Politician or corrupt Lawyer. God is telling you to stop deceiving these people before you leave this world in that state then have to stand before him and give account for all these people's lives; you've destroyed.

This book is dedicated to waking up the conscious of the people that God created in hopes they might turn back to God before it's too late and do it by faith, listening to the message of faith in God & not walking by sight or listening to Corporations, Finances, Politics, Social Groups or Religions of men that deceive you. So God can start marking out your course to be a lamp for your feet & light for your path; then you can see the light of life again and change your image, name, character and become a new creation in God. This is what the messengers were sent to tell you for God, about a new life. (The newness of life in God) So that you would have the chance to be redeemed from yourself, family, crowd & group **because walking with God is not a group thing; it's a very personal & individual thing between you & God**/so don't forget.

Because when you stand before God, no one will be there with you/to share their opinion or advice.

"THROUGH THE STORM"

God will ask you did you figure it out and the answer better be; **God was worthy to be praised** because he was with me till the end. God never abandon me, I turned away from God and listen to a lesser advice that got me in all this trouble; I'm in today. (Please forgive me father for not loving you the way; I should have.)

The Bible says: be quick to listen, slow to speak and slow to become angry because anger does not bring about the life that God desires. Trust in the Lord with all your heart, mind, strength and soul because God is trying to lead you to a blessing.

"RELIGIOUS CONFUSION"

Religion or Spirituality **you choose**, my friends here is where the confusion starts. Now that you understand there's a difference between right & wrong, good & evil and you don't want to be on the worldly side any more. You know, you want to repair your relationship with God. You usually start with choosing a religion (**no matter what the name**) there all manmade and not of God, but of this world.

Spirituality is of God, even though you can't see God; he exists and you know in your heart there's a God. God has revealed himself to the person by his spirit and now the person must start to move in Gods direction by faith.

People begin getting caught up in many religious functions, by which they come in by faith, but quickly turn their faith into religion and start walking by sight. They start adopting manmade rules & regulations to govern their lives then begin building buildings & incorporating people with titles to control them based on how much they can give or not give (**not based on the spirit of God**), but if they agree with their manmade rules or not, skin color, clothing, status & position in life.

"RELIGIOUS CONFUSION"

All these things begin to develop in churches and most of the leadership & congregation are usually one dimensional, there all White, Black, Asian or Hispanic; you get my point and rarely are the races mixed together; especially at the top. Usually the leaders in the pulpit are of the same race because it's a corporation or family business trying to lead the people by their own ways to get their money. (They don't listen to God)

Jesus says: "my family is those who do the will of God" not my natural family or race.

You go in truly seeking God, but eventually find out you're hooked too & part of something, that's not from God. God is trying to make you aware of it, but the manipulation & persuasion is so strong in these buildings; it's hard to resist them because they have set their ways above Gods ways. God is telling you to do something, but they're telling you something else. They tell you, it's better to listen to them & be part of their group/than to listen & walk with God. The outcome is the spiritual person is eventually cast out for speaking against the manmade things going on like (**Stephen** in **Acts Chapter 6 & 7**).

"RELIGIOUS CONFUSION"

Jesus says: "you travel around the world to win a single convert, only to make him twice as much the son of hell as you are" (Matthew 23: 15) **Read Mt Chapter 23.**

I find many people who are religious in nature that God super naturally saved from situations in their life and know only God could have saved them. (I find them now to be the most critical people in life, who don't even believe in miracles any more, but believe in their manmade rules & traditions.)These people were not following rules when God saved them by faith, but now force others to follow tradition by sight.

It happens in every generation, people follow their own ways. When Noah was building the Ark, no one would help him. It says God was upset with most of the people of that generation because their ways were corrupt. Because Noah was an individual who listened to God all the time; they thought he was crazy and said that's not normal; especially when God told him to build the Ark.

They were too busy partying, marrying & being given in marriage when the door of the Ark was shut up and the floods came then many of them were destroyed and only a few were saved. Those few, who listened to God and believed before the rain came/were saved. Jesus says: **blessed are those that don't have to see to believe**.

"RELIGIOUS CONFUSION"

We see it in the story of Lot when he left Abraham to go live & listen to the city people of Sodom; instead of listening to the good advice of Abraham who was a man of faith. Who did not always know where he was going, but knew God was leading & guiding him into a blessing. Abraham's blessings & relationship with God was so strong that when Lots people started quarrelling with him over material things; Abraham said take whatever you want and go. Because Lot did not recognize his blessing was from being around Abraham. His clan wanted to leave with the material things because they had a selfish & religious nature; thinking Lot had everything figured out at this point and he knew more than Abraham. Abraham said, if you choose the right then I will go left; but if you choose left then I will go right;

"Why do you think Abraham told Lot (you choose) and I will go in the opposite direction" because Abraham knew no matter which direction he went; God was with him not Lot. (A leader of greedy quarrelers or trouble makers for gain/Gen 13:7) So Lot went and later Abraham had to rescue him from Sodom. (Gen 14:12)

"RELIGIOUS CONFUSION"

When God was going to destroy Sodom & Gomorrah, he stopped and told Abraham what he was going to do. **Why does God need to tell Abraham anything?** It's because God warns us before destruction. God tries to tell us not to be in places; he doesn't want us to be in. Because when it's time for that place to be destroyed; God doesn't want you there. (Gen 18:16-21)

That's how it was in the book of Habakkuk; God said there's a group of evil people coming that are Gods to themselves. They're going to try and destroy everything & everybody in their path. Habakkuk said Lord, why do my eyes have to see this. God said get out of their way & get on your porch and write it down. I'm (God) telling you what's going to happen, but you're going to be alright.

God tells us in the book of Daniel, that the whole world is corrupt; they will continue to be evil and continue to do wrong, but I want you to continue walking with God. God tells Daniel continue doing what you've been doing; walking with God & don't worry because your days are already set and I have prepared a place for you. You're going to be alright. (Dan 12:9-13)

"SALVATION"

My friends, they start out with good intensions, but sooner or later; they're corrupted by this world with its desires that deceive them into taking their eyes off God. They quit believing in the power of God to transform people's lives, minds & hearts to become a new person that walks with God apart from the group.

But there are some messengers & Evangelist, that are loyal & dedicated to God; their mission is to do all that God has asked them to do. God has people moving around doing things that you wouldn't expect them to be doing, but they're doing it all for the glory of God, love, peace, kindness, goodness, fairness and justice. They're super-naturally intervening in the darkness to bring people into the understanding of the way, truth, life, love and light of God; so they're not hardened by this world because this world has hardened some of the people's hearts.

The scriptures say; **be careful that sin does not harden your heart & turn you away from God.** (Heb 3:7-19)

"SALVATION"

My friends, I'm warning you today; when God gets a hold of you, continue to pray & trust in God, continue to read and seek wisdom & understanding though it cost all you have; then God will continue to lead & guide you to a blessing. God will surround you with people & things, he wants to be around you and he will weed out people & things, he doesn't want around you; according to his word, way and goodness that he has planned for your life. (It will be unmistakable & undeniable when you see things coming & going; you will know that God is in control of your life.)

You will see people trying to stop you from listening to God; that's how you will know, but people who love God will rejoice with you in your salvation! Those who love God & truth will know you're walking with God and no weapon formed against you will prosper because God is on your side. They will know you have & believe in the "power of God" even in the worst of times.

"SALVATION"

I'm explaining the process & confusion the individual will go through, just before they're about to be saved. The beginning of salvation (as a baby believer) the individual starts to hear God more & more each day, (Like the boy Samuel) but there was a time you couldn't hear God at all. Like Peter says; you once swindled people for a living before the salvation of God came. (When God was not in your life)

Now you're a new creation or person in God, but what you didn't anticipate was the devil coming as an angel of light sitting in the pulpit deceiving many. When John the Baptist was about to be beheaded and knew he had prepared the way for the Lord; He sent a message to ask Jesus are you the one to come or should we expect another. Jesus answered, what did you go out to see; a man dressed in fine clothes sitting in the high seat/no, but a prophet and much more!

Not someone sitting in the pulpit trying to control everyone else, **but someone moving around trying to save souls & people from destruction.** Jesus said; if you don't believe in me/at least believe in the miracles, you see me do for the glory of God. (He made people see & walk toward the truth, so they could be saved)

"EVANGELISM or CHURCH you choose"

Either you believe in reaching out to save others or you believe in building worship. No one can serve two kingdoms. This information will help you choose correctly.

Even though there are temples all around that display no power to heal or save those falling through the cracks of life. John the Baptist knew; Jesus answer was the truth.

The scriptures tell us; the man of God will come with the spirit & power of God. His word will be a double edge sword to divide soul & spirit, bone & marrow; his word will either make your heart leap for joy & praise God or make you angry & hate God. Jeremiah says; the word of God is offensive to them.

Because many of them have fell in love with their positions & titles in religion, banking, corporations, politics, & court rooms; they will put men to death to protect their titles in this world. They will crucify your name, character, dignity, word & life to destroy you, but God will lift you up as soon as you separate yourself from them. (So people start church hopping) They start going to Baptist, Pentecostal, Methodist, Sanctified, Catholic & Muslim until they go to church after church searching for something; they will never find **because what they're looking for can't be found in a building**.

"EVANGELISM or CHURCH you choose"

God is in control of the whole world and he can't be contained in buildings because **God is spirit and those who worship him must worship him in spirit & truth!** God already knows you're searching & looking, so he keeps bringing people and things in & out of your life until you get to a point/where you realize or understand; you can't do it by sight, but it must be done by faith. (You're not in control, so walk with God)

If your husband or wife leaves you, don't worry because God will replace them with someone better that believes and it will be a blessing for you. Don't over react when someone leaves you and kill everyone because God wants to put something better in your life. Someone you can fellowship with at home and rejoice in your relationship with God & be happy about life.

"EVANGELISM or CHURCH you choose"

When you lose good friends, don't worry because God is going to replace them with better friends that can keep you walking with God.

If you lose a boy friend or girl friend, don't worry or get frustrated & take your life because God is going to give you someone else that will make you praise & thank God; you held on and waited.

If you have to leave your church because you don't think everything going on there is right and you get cast out or kicked out of church (**like Jesus says will happen too many of you**) then don't worry, know God has not left you; he's still with you.

God is trying to use you for the truth to understand we are not about leading people to buildings, but to God. So people will believe in God by spirit & truth and walk by faith not by sight.

Jesus says blessed are those that don't have to see to believe.

(You get my point)

"THE NEW LIFE"

See my friends, I'm about to lead you into a new life. Where the people God put into your life will help you praise & believe in God and their generally happy that you're blessed & not cursed. Not like the old life that you come from where you had jobs, houses, cars, money, friends, husbands & wives, but most of the time they criticized your relationship with God. They nitpicked at your time spent with God. They didn't understand why you read the bible, always prayed, talk with God, walk with God & loved God; they only loved you because of what you did for them, because you provided things, money, houses, cars and parties, but they loved you for all the wrong reasons.

They should have loved you because God was in you. So don't worry because in the new life; God is in you & in the people around you. Now everyone understands why you need God & so do they. You all understand that if things & people are placed above God; they will be stripped & removed from you, but when God is your first love; there's rejoicing instead of arguing and peace instead of confusion.

"THE NEW LIFE"

God is first not last, so we can rejoice in the truth and be happy for one another. So happy that we can testify and give someone a word of encouragement that will change their life by leading them to God. The scripture says; encourage one another daily. Even though all the confusion, past problems & troubles are hard when you come from the unsaved life, **once you know & start walking with God in the new life; your joy is better than sorrow and living in peace is so much better than living in hate.** Amen

You've come to the spirit & glory of the living God that's shining on you!

It's in your heart, mind, thoughts and your thankful that God has restored you & gave you common sense, wisdom and understanding that's above this world. (The scripture says: get wisdom & understanding though it cost all you have) It's time you understand your rightful place with God because God has changed your life at the right moment & time by putting love in your heart for God & people; so you can be taken away in this state because you're right with God to dwell in heaven.

"THE NEW LIFE"

It's important to know the old you could not enter into heaven because of hate & discord for God & people. (Confusion in your heart)

That's why Jesus says; love your enemies & pray for those who use you because they don't know what they're doing. They don't know God like believers do; so pray they find this love of God because it's this love, they seek even though; they don't know it yet. That's why Jesus says; seek & you shall find, knock & the door shall be opened, ask & you shall receive. Everyone who seeks must do so/not for gain, desire or selfishness, but for truth that sets you free from the world. You will be genuinely thankful, happy and humble before God then you can look at sinners & say, blessed be the name of the Lord because God saved me, he can save them too; if they listen to the message. Pray many find God before they leave this world because the day you found God; your life changed forever!

God is not willing for any to parish, but hope all come to have ever lasting life**. The problem is not with God, but with the individual's choice to choose God or the World.** I pray, you choose God over the world.

"BRIDGING THE GAP"

Since I have thoroughly explained to you the individual spirit; **Walking With God: a Personal Relationship.** Now I'm going to bring you to the group or family setting: **And This Is Love: A Spiritual Guide.** I'm about to explain the gap that exists between the individual & family life and what brings them both together. This will make you a well rounded person and bring you full circle; so your joy will be made complete. **God is love**.

My friend, if you love then God is in you and if you don't love, it's because God's love is not in you and you've chosen the world over God. The scripture tells us love is not a new command, but an old command from the very beginning to love God and your neighbor as yourself. (Love the Lord your God with all your heart, mind, strength & soul and love your neighbor as yourself) All scriptures and commands come from this message because God was trying to warn the people, he created (All people) that without his spirit of love**; they wouldn't be able to get along & co-exist in the world he made**.

"BRIDGING THE GAP"

They would ultimately destroy one another. My friend, God fore knew this and placed it in your heart before you ever came into the world as a seed that would be nurtured & blossom at the right time to save your life. (God is going to awaken your spirit at just the right moment & time to give you an opportunity to choose good or evil, life or death) Also God knew that his creation (people) would attempt to create a new way & put it above his ways by inventing organizations like: Religions, corporations, banking, politics and courtrooms to institute those changes at every level of society. (**Little by little they weeded God out**) They took God out of their politics, courtrooms, businesses, churches and homes; they thought everything would be ok and stay together without God even though God was warning them that his spirit was the glue of life and nothing stays together without him, but **they didn't pay attention to God**.

God watches what people do at all times to stop the wicked & bless the righteous.

"BRIDGING THE GAP"

So let me tell you what happened to them, without God in their life; they began to decay from the inside out, their bodies withered, their hearts & minds were darkened. They became foolish, senseless & hopeless without love and the world grew cold & calculating then schemers were born.

They turned on one another until trickery & deceit became a way of life, but it was actually death in disguise as they began to fool & lie to one another to steal each other's possessions. This was happening at every level in every area of life; including churches because the devil comes as an angel of light to steal, kill and destroy people. (**They lost everything and their economy collapsed**)

They retrained everyone to deny God and be lovers or idol worshippers of money & possessions. (**The love of money is the root of all evil**) They thought their husbands, wives, houses, cars & possessions would be kept, but they were sadly mistaken and it didn't work out the way they planned. It never works out the way they plan without God because Gods watching their motives to see, if there good or evil.

"BRIDGING THE GAP"

The **scripture says: apart from God you can do nothing**. Then everything around them collapsed and the world they created crumbed because it was all an illusion, lie & ponzie scheme like: Bernie Madoff from the top down. (From the White House to Street Level or Government to Gangs) They began to destroy, ruin and kill one another to stop the lies from coming out, but it was all revealed to everyone; **they had been deceived**. So they lost their husbands, wives, boyfriends, girlfriends, houses, cars and every nice thing they accumulated or stored up then they lost their minds and lives.

(God tried to warn them of this outcome from the beginning, but they wouldn't pay attention to God then as a last chance; God sent messengers to save them like Noah, Elijah, Jesus, Martin Luther King Jr. and myself—Evangelist John Dye)

I've come that you might know the truth and this truth will set you free from this corrupt world. You're in the world/not of the world; **you belong to God**.

"BRIDGING THE GAP"

That's why this book is being wrote, it's an account of events happening to make you aware & wake you up; so the truth will be in the world, long after I'm gone back to God. In order to stop falsehood from deceiving everybody including the elect, God sent me to write it down, make DVDs & CDs as a testimony to the truth of the will, love and way of God; so the children coming into the world & those who have an ear to hear might be saved. Saved from themselves, society & their own ways; in hope they might turn back to God before it's too late. Because as long as you're a live; you have a chance, but you can't wait on anybody. You must turn back now when the message is heard. You can't wait on your, family, husband, wife, friends, race, boss, co-workers or pastor, you've got to make the choice for yourself; if you want to leave this old life of idol worship & falsehood behind you because it can never lead you to a blessing, peace, happiness or contentment unless you cross over to this new life with God. Where you understand that "God is love" & God would never leave or forsake you, but is telling you the truth that **this is love a spiritual guide**.

"BRIDGING THE GAP"

You walk by faith not by sight, it's something done in the heart not the outward appearance because God's guiding you to this life and surrounding you with every good thing for your happiness & well being. This is a divine spiritual moment in your life; it's an awakening as God removes every bad or evil thing away from you.

It's one on one between you & God, understand this message; I'm giving you today. Read this book from beginning to end, so you can conclude this message is from heaven and the very words of God for life & salvation. **God bless the reader of this book!**

"MIDDLE GROUND"

Before we continue into "**And This Is Love: A Spiritual Guide**" let me point out some important information related to the middle ground of coming from the individual life style to the family or group setting. This is an example of spiritual life and God's love.

The first principle is to understand the concept of giving & receiving; in the beginning a person has the desire to give, but gives with wrong motives expecting something in return. After they give, give, give then don't receive something in return, it hardens or breaks their heart and they don't give anymore. The same thing happens with love; people love, love, love and think they deserve something in return, but when they don't get it. They stop loving. Their hearts start being corrupted then they begin to hate & not love anymore. Their character & hearts become cold or dark; because you can't give with wrong motives that are not sincere.

The scriptures say: if you give, **give with a glad & joyful heart**. (Expect nothing in return) **It's better to give than receive.** It's a blessing to be in a situation where you can give & help someone, but selfish people are rarely in a position to bless others because they don't understand this concept.

You have to have the spirit of God to understand giving and love at its highest level. (Complete Joy)

"MIDDLE GROUND"

It's important to get both of my other books: "**Walking With God: A Personal Relationship"** & "**And This Is Love: A Spiritual Guide"** by Evangelist John Dye to complete your spiritual growth, but this new book; "**Your Personal Destiny: A Complete Guide"** by Evangelist John Dye has both books in it.

God was telling us that people can be converted to the dark side without his spirit and lack the power to resist evil; even though they want to do good/they can't carry out the desire. God was trying to warn people that without his spirit & power, you can't carry out the desire of good; like giving & love. Even though, you want to do it because you see others doing it and it seems right & makes them happy, but **when you do it; it makes you mad because your motives are wrong when doing it**.

When you have the spirit of God in the new life, you give and expect nothing in return because you know/that you can't out give God or love more than God, but it's good to be like God. When you look at your life, it seems like the more you give the more God gives to you and you could really never repay God for all he has done for you! Even though you don't understand it fully in the physical world, but in the spiritual realm, you know God exist and watches all the good your doing then repays you for it because he loves you; even though you don't deserve it all the time.

"MIDDLE GROUND"

So much good is happening to you so often, you realize the person you helped is not the same person that helps you and that's ok because you understand; how the spirit of God works on your behalf for good, but unbelievers don't. Someone walks up and gives you something that will help you because they see the Good & God in you. So blessings start coming from many different directions & people. (Miracles)

You have so many blessings that you keep on giving because there's a joy that comes from giving that you don't feel from receiving. The receiver has a beggar feeling/while the giver feels good about being able to help someone in need & expect nothing in return because they understand the value of having God in their life.

So it is with love, you love not because someone loves you, but because you know God loves you and his spirit is in you to love others. You know God saved you many times from destruction, so you go & love those who are unlovable in hopes that God will save them; if they have an ear to hear the message! You attempt to explain to the un-Godly, how the love & wisdom of God is higher than the love & knowledge of this world for salvation. (Eternity, life with God)

"GOD IS GREAT"

Above all things God is great!

The great love of God doesn't love you because of what you do or don't do, but what you believe or don't believe. (The scriptures say: believe in God, believe also in me) One must believe that God exists and he rewards those/who diligently seek him. God loves you because he made you and wants you to understand his ways. Because if you understand his ways; you will be saved from the corruption of the world. If you understand Gods ways are higher than your ways, you will not be converted to the dark side of hate & confusion.

Example:

There's a family with three children, let's use the older child as the bad kid; we know most parents love their children the same at least we would hope. Now the older child is breaking all the rules of the house. The parents talk to the child, but the child starts making excuses about the behavior and blaming the parents like: you don't love me; you love my brother & sister more than me. The child continues to rant & rave about how unfair life is in the house, but failing to look at its own ways.

"GOD IS GREAT"

The parents talk to the child with the love of God in their heart and says; listen & pay attention to what I'm about to tell you. We love all our children the same, but you're trying to manipulate and use our love to get your own ways.

You're trying to position yourself in our house to do wrong, but we are not allowing it to happen because you're selfish. God told us to establish good rules for everyone to get along and enjoy peace, happiness, contentment, spirit of love, truth and blessings in this house. You're trying to break those rules & convince everybody here to do things your way, but you're going to come back to your senses because this is our house.

We've been watching you for awhile, you've been drifting to the dark side and you don't treat your brother & sister like you should. In fact, you've been mistreating & deceiving them, you've been tricking them out of their possessions, leading them down the wrong path and they're starting to pick up your ways. It's just a matter of time before God finds out what you're doing and he's going to take you away from here. We love you and we don't want to see you go, but **God's coming and he will not stand for this kind of manipulation.**

"GOD IS GREAT"

We know the children belong to God and the Lord gives & takes away; he allows us a little time to train them in the Lord. Let us tell you why, God is going to take you away from us because we have a bigger job than you know. Our job is to love the other two kids in this house and not let you corrupt them; so they can live & study in peace. Our job is to train them in the way they should go, like we loved & trained you before you went astray. We are not allowing you to break every rule, corrupt everybody and turn everyone against each other in our house.

God's telling us to pray for you and hope that you get it then come back to the light, knowledge and truth of what we are telling you today. If you continue on this path, you will surely be taken away and probably end up in jail or worse. You will find yourself somewhere other than this loving atmosphere, God has provided because you refused to listen. You're rebelling against everything; God has surrounded & blessed you with for living a good life **because you can't understand the truth.**

"GOD IS GREAT"

Result:

Eventually something happens and God takes the child away, **so the rest of the family can live in peace!** The child goes to jail as an example, in fact the child goes to jail two or three times before they get it or begin to understand the truth. The child starts to reflect on the message, the parents were telling from the beginning until now, about the way, love, truth, understanding and wisdom of God. The child starts to understand, you don't put your ways above Gods ways because it will lead to trouble that gets you taken away.

Now the child is older, gets released from jail and gets an apartment to establish a new life apart from the parents; then call the parents over to the new apartment and says: mom & dad, I'm sorry for the way, I was living my life, for the confusion, I caused in your house, all the things I did to my brother & sister, for putting my ways above the houses ways & Gods ways; you were trying to instill in me.

"GOD IS GREAT"

I want the rules of my place to be similar to yours because I'm having my first child. Now, I understand/what you were trying to tell me and I have an opportunity to tell my child the way to go.

I can only pray that my apartment enjoys the peace, love, truth, tranquility and spirit of God like your house. I know that you were right & I was wrong, God was right & I was wrong because God wants me to choose right over wrong. I want to have a house of peace not confusion, so my child will have a chance at a decent and good life. Thank you, thank God and pray for me & my house because I need a Bible. The parents say: praise God and we will buy you a Bible for the apartment!

My friends, I hope you understand this message because this is what God is trying to do for your individual life and family. I bless you in your new life as you continue to walk with God, even, if you have to walk alone. Pray that God surrounds you with people that will walk with you, so in the end when you stand before God; he will say: well done, good and faithful servant; you kept the faith & believed even though you didn't see.

(God bless the reader of this book)

"GOD'S FIRST/NOT LAST"

My friends in every generation, God have sent true messengers like myself to warn the people, but they fall short of the glory of God because they won't listen to the message.

The people gather around themselves a great number of preachers & priest of religions that tell them what they're itching ears wanted to hear! Until death creeps into their lives in many forms then multitudes of people are destroyed by following the crowd and listing to bad advice & gimmicks.

Men like me come into the world to help & warn you, when times are bad and the people are far from God. Noah came when God was upset with most of the people of his generation, Elijah came to warn the people with great power & Spirit, Jesus came with great love & compassion, but his own people rejected his wisdom then crucified him and Martin Luther King came to lead with unity & peace, but was shot down in violence by the people of his generation.

Jesus says: Since the beginning, they have been killing Gods prophets from Abel to Zechariah and this generation will be held accountable. (Luke 11:50-51) **But I say: it has been done from the beginning to now, that's the truth!**

"GOD'S FIRST/NOT LAST"

Friends, never forget this is about walking with God every day!

Enoch walked with God many years, had children and he was known to be a friend of God then God took him away.

The Bible says, David was a Shepherd boy of humble beginnings, who became King and God was with him. David had many writings in the Bible of wisdom & understanding, but Psalms 23 tells us, what was in his heart.

Psalms 23:

The Lord is my shepherd, I will not want for anything. He makes me lie down in green pastures; he leads me beside quiet waters and restores my soul.

He guides me in paths of righteousness for his name's sake even though I walk through the valley of the shadow of death; I will fear no evil because you are with me and your rod & staff comforts me.

You prepare a table before me in the presence of my enemies anoint my head with oil and my cup over flows; surely goodness, mercy and love will follow me all the days of my life and I will dwell in the house of the Lord forever.

"GOD'S FIRST/NOT LAST"

Daniel 12:9-13

Daniel tells us, People were wicked and the daily sacrifice to God was abolished or stopped and they set up an abomination that causes desolation that destroyed the people; It was the end of that generation & religion, but God tells him to go his own separate way because he is highly favored and will receive his reward or crown in heaven.

2Timothy 4:3-8

The scriptures tell us, that there was a man, who preached the truth to the congregation, but God told him to pack all of his belongings then leave and do the work of an Evangelist. You will receive a crown in heaven for all the hardship you faced on earth. (Because people didn't want to hear, truth in the congregation)

All these scriptures tell the people on earth to put God first not last, regardless of what, they're going through. (Trials & Tribulations)

David, Daniel, Paul, John & all the sons of God mentioned earlier, have one message: It's ok to go to church, but never let it confuse you about the truth/**your home is the house of God** and you should worship & praise God daily from home/**your body is the temple of God** and you should take care of it & worship God in your heart **because the kingdom of heaven is within you.**

"GOD'S FIRST/NOT LAST"

You get one chance at life to see, if you will serve God or the world.

No one can serve two kingdoms because you will love one & hate the other.

Evangelist John Dye says,

Walk with God, endure hardship & heart-ache then stand firm till the end and God will have a place prepared for you with a Crown of Eternal Life.

God bless you all.

"CONCLUSION 1"

Here's the message, no matter what group you're apart off: Family, Business, Religion, Politics or Friends. God is concerned about the individual apart from the groups because God is not willing that any should perish.

Individuals think groups are ok in the beginning, but they don't understand people change their minds along the way. God knows the heart & intent of the heart to do good or evil, God knows when someone has changed their mind toward you and **tries to warn you**, but you refuse to listen because the group or person has deceived you or brain washed you. So you no longer do what's best for you, you do what's best for the group and suffer with everyone else. God is trying to help you make decisions that are best for you and your soul. So you'll be content and happy with your life.

(**The group may not have your best interest at heart, but God always does!**)

He sends the message to save you; if you have an ear to hear the truth!

Please don't be all in with the group, enjoy it for a while **then know when to walk away for your own good** and with God's help you will know when that day comes.

Without God, you will be trapped by your own willingness to follow the crowd insuring your down fall.

"CONCLUSION 1"

1 John 2: 15-17, (below)

Do not love the world or anything in the world. If anyone loves the world, **the love of the Father is not in them**. For everything in the world—the cravings of the sinful person, the lust of their eyes and the boasting of what they have and do—**does not come from the Father**, but from the world. **The world and its desires pass away, but the person who does the will of God lives forever!**

You're in the world/**not of the world**. Enjoy what you have, while you have it because it's a blessing from God and please don't be troubled, if it's taken away because God knows best. (The Lord gives & takes away for your good)

Love & trust Gods decision or message to you the **"Individual".** (Walk with God)

Sincerely with Peace & Love,

Evangelist John Dye

www.heartministriesonline.com

"INTRODUCTION 2"

This book was written not to replace your Holy Bible, but it was written to be in agreement with it; And to spark the spirits fire of the individual reading this book. So that he or she might have a deeper understanding into the truth of God's word (**through love**).

By Author:

Evangelist John Dye

(Man of God)

God bless the reader of this book!

"SPIRITUAL FOUNDATION OF LIFE"

God has put in order a foundation of life that no man can change.

God

Men (who love God)

Women who love (men who love God)

And Children who love (parents who love God)

This is called: **The Blessed Hope!**

"LIVING TO PLEASE GOD"

The blessed hope (**Holy Marriage**) is the state of blessedness in which all the members of the family are born again because God wants to create people for himself (set apart to be like God; loyal, faithful and Holy)

God has said; "I am holy, even so you be holy" So the parents should be born again with the children being trained in the Lord. Then everyone will be able to enter the good life as well as the kingdom of heaven; also your eyes can see a blessing and the kingdom of heaven then you will be able to hear Gods voice and walk in spirit and truth.

And this is love as found in the scriptures as the truth to the Fathers glory, in his Sons and the Holy Spirit.

"VICTORY"

God has predestined you and the family for glory before the creation of the world.*

The promise is for you and your children and for all who are far off; whom the Lord our God will call.*

Jesus said: "**My family is those who do the will of my father in Heaven**"*

"CREATION"

In the beginning God created the heavens and the earth and everything found in them. And God said: "That it was good!"

Then God said: "Let us create man in our image" (he created man a little lower than the angels) so God made them male and female.

God blessed them and said, "Be fruitful and multiply; be careful to take care of the earth and overcome it."

"PERFECT PEACE"

Then God rested from all his work and looked at what he had created and it was very good! (Perfect)**

God expected the man of God and woman of man, to raise Godly offspring. And continue a legacy of holiness on earth.

(**Heaven on earth**)

"HOLY MARRIAGE"

Now that God has laid out the heavens and earth in relationship to one another according to his will and good pleasure. Paradise is truly a blessed state to remain in because you're in God's presence at all times.

Therefore God blessed the marriage:

God

Men (who love God)

Women who love (men who love God)

And children who love (parents who love God)

This three-strand cord is not easily broken,* what God has joined together let no man separate* (Holy Marriage); especially, two believers of holiness training their children to understand the love of God.

As we move on from here we see further evidence of Gods order and God holding everyone accountable to keeping the order!*

"GOD GIVEN AUTHORITY"

So God said, that he had created this perfect life style called "**Paradise**", but there was no one to take care of it.

So he put man in charge of it (to take care of it and work it) to make it fruitful.*

And God said, "To the man in the garden of paradise, of every tree here you may freely eat, but of the tree of the knowledge of good and evil you must not eat, for the day you eat of this tree you will **surely die**!*"

"OBEDIENCE"

So at this point, we see God has given us some commands to follow let us point out these commands.

- **One**: God commands us to raise children in the Lord. **(Godly offspring)***

- **Two**: God commands us to take care of what he has given us and to take care of what he has given us to live on (the earth and the **blessings of paradise**).*

- **Three**: God commands us to be content with what he has provided and not to seek our own understanding, but rely on God. **(Faith)****

"WORKING FOR GOD"

Now God trusts the man, he put in charge because God has given the man his spirit; when God breathed into his nostrils the breath of life.

(That's truly life to live with God in his presence).

Then man became a living being.*

Since man has the Holy Spirit, God allows the man to name everything and whatever the man named it that was its name!*

"A HELP MATE"

And God said, "It's not good for man to be alone." (Now it's important to note that up to this point the man of God is faithfully doing everything just as God has commanded him).

So God decides to make him a woman and God brings the woman to him to see what the man would name her. The man names her woman/bone of his bone. (Meaning one flesh)*

Note: **God did not name the woman** (The man did)!

At this point, we see God did not go behind the man's back and re-name anything, that's not God's character to double cross.

God does not lie or change his order of life.

So God tells the couple to move away from their kinfolks and then two have indeed become one flesh in the unity of love in paradise.*

"SPIRITUAL FOUNDATION OF MARRIAGE"

So we see God has established his foundation of life in **paradise for good living**.

God as the head of the marriage mainly (man),
Man as the head of the (woman),
And Parents as the head of the (children), mainly woman.*

One: We see man will be blessed, if he listens to God.*

Two: Woman will be blessed, if she listens to her man of God. (Husband)*

Three: Children will live long and be blessed, if they obey their (Godly Parents).*

"THE REASON/REBELLION"

Now here is where the problem comes in. You know, when everything is going good something has to happen!
(There is a reason for this.)

The reason is about the time God put everything in order on earth, which occupied most of his time because God does things right the first time.

God left three angels in charge of heaven. (Arc-angels)**

One: Michael – in charge of the army of God. (Faithful)*

Two: Gabriel – in charge of the messages of God. (Diligent)*

Three: Lucifer – in charge of the praises of God. (Loyalty)*

The problem is Lucifer got tired, envious, jealous, proud, arrogant, selfish, rebellious and rude. **Lucifer did not want to be loyal anymore, so Lucifer convinced a group of angels to rebel against heaven and Gods commands.***

"DECEIVER 1"

To be truthful, Lucifer was not carrying out half of Gods commands and Lucifer knew that God was going to eventually check on him. Sooner or later (it was just a matter of time).*

God was going to find out Lucifer had not kept his word. And Lucifer was going to be out of heaven for **lying to God continuously**.*

Lucifer did not want to go alone (because misery loves company).

So before anyone could find out what he was up too, Lucifer deceived some other angels and convinced them God was not worthy to be praised or to receive the glory and honor do him.*

"TRIAL"

God did get around to checking on his kingdom, (heaven and the angels) only to find out that one of his angels had been mocking him, lazy and tricking all the other angels into disobedience.*

Then God called for Michael and Gabriel top angels in heaven (to be fair and establish the facts by two or three witnesses.)*

God wanted to know, what should be done to Lucifer for the rebellion he has caused?

"VERDICT"

There was only one conclusion to banish Lucifer from heaven, so no other angel would learn his ways.

So God commanded Michael to take an army of angels and put heaven back in order. Do whatever it takes, but **restore order and glory to heaven.** **

"WAR IN HEAVEN"

Michael and his angels fought against Lucifer and his angels. The result: **Lucifer and his angels lost their place in heaven** and they were hurled down to the earth.

Gabriel speaks, "Woe to you people on earth because Lucifer (now called Satan because of his rebellious and un-loyal nature) has been cast down around you. **Satan is full of fury because he knows that his time is short.**"*

"SATAN'S VIEW/FALSE PROPHET"

God knew that Satan would attempt to deceive his creation. Satan would try to twist the word of God around (because Satan was around God everyday).

Therefore Satan says: that's not what God meant. He tells people God is not worthy to be praised every day. Satan tells them to take time to glorify themselves and have fun. (That's what God meant)

Satan says: **I know because I used to be with God.** **

"UNGODLY VIEW"

People should ask the Question why isn't (Satan) with God now, but **people simply go along with Satan's lies because they want to be independent**.

They (people) want to be their own God. People want power, money, glory and to be in control of their own lives.*

Notice: I did not say (**self-control**). There is a real difference as you will soon see!

"TEMPTATION"

Back to earth, paradise and the frustration, that comes with the Devil or Satan being allowed to tempt the people of God.*

The reason: God has put heaven in order!
Now everybody who enters heaven must first be tested to see, **if their faithful to God** or choose Satan and his followers.*

Note: Satan is also called the Devil.*

We will switch names here to (Devil).
At this point, we are giving the woman the benefit of not knowing the difference because the enemy will change names and masquerade as an angel of light.*

The woman not knowing the difference that both names have the same meaning. (It's still the ancient serpent called the Devil or Satan) **that attempts to lead the whole world astray**.*

"TEMPTATION"

As the woman was roaming through the garden of paradise, she met the Devil and the Devil asked her. What were the rules for Paradise?*

So the woman told the Devil. We may eat from any tree in the garden, but not from the tree in the middle of the garden and you must not touch it or you will die.

At this point, we see some things going on here. I don't believe the woman sounded to convincing to the Devil because keep in mind the Devil knows the word too!*

The Devil knew, that the woman left out the word (free), she add the word (touch) and she made it sound as if they (might die) not surely die!*

Note: **How important it is to study God's word as a family**.

"IMPORTANCE OF KNOWING GODS WORD"

The Devil knew from conversations with the woman, that she did not run away immediately or say ask (my husband) because he knows the word better than me!*

One: that's why God gave the woman a man of God. The man is the spiritual head of the family. The man is commanded to study the scriptures daily and to mediate on them day and night. **

Two: God's word tells us to cast down every imagination that sets itself up against the kingdom of heaven or paradise on earth.*

Three: God tells us not to lean to our own understanding and knowledge because it puffs up our mind and puts us in danger of falling from glory. (**The good life**)*

"DISOBEDIENCE"

So the woman did eat from the forbidden tree and she gave some to her husband. I'm convinced (this was not the first time) she had ate from this tree and then deceived and lead her husband into sin. (More than likely by her lying to him as the devil had lied to her.)*

We see this same sinful nature (way too often) in our society today to dismiss, what I'm saying.
D.N.A evidence has proven this to be true.*

Note: In this section, there is a repeat performance just as Satan had tried to deceive God earlier in heaven by not keeping his word or doing his job. (Praising God)

Satan does it again, but this time it's the woman on earth; The Devil is deceiving and teaching deceit too.*

The Devil did not go to the (man of God) first. He used the weaker mate. (Woman)

"DECEIVER 2"

The immediate result of sin is to deceive others by lying because you know the truth is going to come out. (Sooner or later)*

So people try to hide from one another, but the problem is you can't hide from God. God sees all things even the hidden things or those things done in the dark.*

After all that deceit, God came and ask for the man in charge.*

"THE BLAME GAME"

So immediately the blame game starts and God goes down through his chain of command. (Godly order)

- Man of God first
- Woman of man second
- And eventually the serpent. (Devil/Satan)*

God also tells them the effect sin and deceit will have on their future children. (Turmoil and hostility)*

Note: That same turmoil and hostility are found in many books of the bible and families today.*

Godly order:

God
Man of God
Woman of (Godly man)
Children of (Godly parents)
Satan (the tempter)

At this point, God still does not change the rules. God puts them away from the tree of immortality or life for now!*

Note: The man of God fell to the peer pressure from the world around him. (Instead of maintaining his testimony and protecting what God had gave him by calling on God first)*

"THE BLAME GAME"

- No weapon formed against you shall prosper.*
- If God is for us who can be against us.*
- My God will deliver me from all my troubles.*
- Everyone who calls on the name of the lord shall be saved.*

Note: **The messages of God are to be understood and you are to hold on to his promises**. (Patience)

"GODLY DISCIPLINE"

We see God tells the (**man**) because you listen to your wife, now life is going to be hard for you and your family.
(Filled with confusion and hardships)*

God tells the (woman) because you listen to the serpent/Devil (This thing you've done!)* Your desire is going to be for your husband. Your husband will rule over you and you will have much pain in your life. (Especially through your children)*

God tells the serpent (devil) from now on there will be (spiritual) war between the children of God and the children of the Devil with the (woman) caught in the middle of the mess!*

Note: **War means no agreement between the children of God and the children of the Devil**.*

Note: Now notice, I did not say man of God. (I only said "**man**")

This is a **worldly marriage** (not a Holy marriage) because people are moving away from Gods presences (not toward God as they should.)

"LISTENING TO UNGODLINESS"

It's not even good to be un-equally yoked with un-believers because of the danger of what we listen to on a daily basis.

We must be conscious of it at all times. (Guard yourself spiritually)*

Half of our friends should not be un-believers and God forbid, if all of our friends are un-believers. (**That's a person waiting to fall**)*

"FALLING AWAY FROM GOD"

Now **we see sin and rebellion takes us away from God** and we do not live a life filled with all the good promises and the blessings of God! (And not just that)

Sin turns people against one another, especially in marriages and families.

I would have to say; "The love of money, drug abuse and adultery are the biggest contributors to a high divorce rate, family structure break down and overall rebellion against Godliness!*

So we see why God warned us, that it's (not good) too:

- Lean to our own understanding.
- Trust in ourselves alone.
- Or become our own God.

But it's enough to be like God:

- Made in his image.
- Carrying out his commands.
- And understanding his ways.*

"SAY NO/A LESSON LEARNED"

We see the Devil can't wait to attack your marriage because he knows long lasting (**Holy marriages**) produce Godly offspring and Godly people.

Holy marriages are good examples of how, we should live on earth as it is in heaven.

Holy marriages encourage us all to do better and to become better people morally, physically, mentally and spiritually.*

"GOOD ADVICE"

The wisdom of God

Morally: Because it protects our body from sickness and disease, if we obey Gods command of being united in one flesh. (Godly Marriage)*

Physically: Because we Exercise our body producing lovely physiques. (This is the temple of God)*

Mentally: Our affection ought to be on God because it gives us peace of mind in our daily lives. So we should think of praise worthy things. (Heavenly Things)*

Spiritually: Because it teaches us love for God, which binds everything else together with him (God) in this life and the life to come. (Eternity) **And love for one another as well**!*

Since all have fallen short of the glory, that God predestined for us (the good life) in his presence. It only stands to reason, since many have been led astray. Now many must be called.*

Note: The question is asked, who, what, when, where and why did the individual turn away from God.*

"REDEMPTION/THE CALL OF GOD"

Let's talk about God's plan of redemption.
(Bringing people back to God)*
God has thought about it long and hard to come up with the perfect plan.
Are you ready to hear this? (**All must be broken**)
Yes, every knee will bow and tongue confess that the lord is God almighty! If a person does not confess his or her sin and rebellion that person will remain apart from God forever.*

One must believe:

- God is still on the throne and he is in control of heaven and earth.*
- Jesus was sent into the world to save sinners and he was resurrected back to the right hand of God to make intercession for those being saved.*
- Jesus resurrection is for the repentance and forgiveness of sins and proof of life after death.*
- The Holy Spirit is a promise of God from the very beginning.

The Holy Spirit is here to lead you, guide you, convict you, comfort you and lead you into all truth about the righteousness of God.*

Note: **True worshipers are the kind of worshipers; God is looking for because they worship in spirit and truth. God is spirit and his worshipers must worship in spirit and in truth.***

"NEW COVENANT"

God found fault with the first covenant and he established a new covenant the body of an individual. (A personal relationship)

God took it upon himself and he put his laws (words) in their hearts and on their minds. God has established himself as their God and his people, no longer will a man have to teach his neighbor or brother to know the lord because they will all know him from the least to the greatest!

God has promised to forgive their sin because God will teach them.* (Your body is the temple of God)

So God starts drawing people to himself by spirit, miracles, signs and wonders. (Divine intervention)*

Draw near to God and God will draw near to you!*

"MEN AFTER GODS OWN HEART"

God has chosen, men after his own heart (men of God) to go out into the world to look for lost people. (Sheep)*

They (men of God) are to tell the lost people to return home, back to God in paradise with a repentant, remorseful, humble and respectful attitude toward God.*

God is one who judges the thoughts and attitude of the heart. You can't fool God as you do some people. Likewise, you can't fool the one God sends to you because God has equipped the man of God for his Mission.*

"RUNNING FROM GOD"

Now many are called, but **few are chosen**. And all have heard the word, but not everyone wants to hear the word of God. Because the word is offensive to many of them and a burden or a waste of time, that takes away from their own routine!*

The word of God tells us, that men or women are without excuse. The word will be preached and made known to the people of earth.
(Nations)*

"TURNING TO GOD/SALVATION"

Since men and women are stubborn, hard-headed or hard hearted; God sends his beloved sons (messengers) into the world to spread the message of hope to the lost and broken hearted.* **As an example:** God sends Jesus to call sinners to repentance, so the sick can be healed from a broken spirit and a hardened heart toward God. (Bitterness)*

It's down to the now or never stage for the sinner and the sinner is close or near death at this point. Now **God is making a last appeal to save the sinner from his or her own destruction**.* God allows the messenger to deliver the message of hope and redemption, so the sinner can be reconciled or restored to holiness.* (True life) Life in God's presence again. This is called salvation.

Salvation is found in the word of God by faith because Jesus is a representation of God's love for the lost and broken hearted.* **God loves Jesus and God loves you too**!*

"PARABLE OF THE TENANTS"

Now to prove what I'm saying, Remember the story Jesus told about the man who had a large vineyard. The man rented it out to some people and the time came to pay the owner for renting his vineyard. So the owner sent his servant to collect the debt owed, but the users said, (We will not pay) and bandit together to beat the servant.

So the owner sent another servant and they killed him too! The owner sent a third and got the same result. (Stoned to death) Then the owner sent his son and the users said ah! The heir has come let us kill him and take his inheritance.

So now, that the truth has been revealed and the owner knows their heart or (intentions).

Finally the owner came and put an end to those wretched or evil men.

"BELIEVING GODS WORD"

We see God sent his servants into the world. God sent his son as a last appeal then God will come and pass final judgment.

People who use others will end up with nothing not even their lives.

The users had an opportunity to make wealth; pay the owner, live at peace with God and man, but the devil filled their hearts with greed and disrespect.

The scriptures say; **what is it to gain the whole world and lose your soul**.*

God is always fair in every circumstance, but people don't pay attention to God. God gives us plenty of warnings, this is why we put him first (not last)!*

"HISTORY"

God was not unaware of Satan's schemes. God sent his son Jesus to tell the world about the greatest power on earth and in heaven. (**Love**)!

God so loved the world, he gave his only begotten son, that whoever believes in him will not perish (be destroyed), but have eternal life.*

God warns us, that whatever we do should be done in the light and in his presence (for God and through God)!*

The world did not want to hear the Son (Jesus) or the message of Love! (**They hated Jesus without reason**) They killed him because they did not want their actions to be exposed.*

"PUTTING YOUR HOUSE IN ORDER"

All throughout creation or history; God has chosen men to warn and save people with the same message.*

Repent for the kingdom of heaven is near, so turn around (straighten up)
And put your house in order.

If God had to put heaven in order (and we are made in his likeness) then we must put our house in order as it is in heaven.*

"PERSECUTION"

These messengers from Abel down to Jesus have been righteous men, faithful and loyal. **These dedicated men of God risk their lives for the word of God and your salvation**. (They were ridiculed, punished and killed.)*

"EQUALITY"

Jesus said, "There will be men who come after him, that will do greater things than he did!"*

There have been a few men, (we should mention) who risked their lives for righteous causes. Such as:
(The Disciples, Gandhi, Abraham Lincoln, Martin Luther King Jr., Nelson Mandela and many more not mentioned.)

These great men deserve our applause, but it all happened because **God loved the world and loved us first**.*

"ENDURANCE/TRUSTING GOD"

We truly owe thanks to Jesus, who set the wheels of endurance into motion. Jesus endured opposition from sinful or evil men to the point of death on the cross.*

Jesus resisted the Devil by the word of God and his testimony. **He laid down his life** to be totally used by God the Father.*

"SUBMISSION"

We see Jesus was not willing to take or settle for less than what God desired for life. (Meaning to live in God's presence forever)

Jesus was made a little lower than the angels to carry out his mission with faithfulness, loyalty and diligence to the very end to bring God the Father (**God almighty**) the glory he deserves!*

Now Jesus is the author and finisher of our faith and Jesus has been seated at the right hand of God with angels, authority and powers in submission to him.*

There's a place with God for everyone who believes!

"LOYALTY"

Now we see not even the mightiest angel was able to do what Jesus did.
(To prove God's point)

God wanted us to understand the reason; he created man for himself.
(Man is God's glory)

Jesus did remain faithful in human form, that's how awesome God is my friends!
God already knew, what the devil was up to and created man to praise him!*

Remember Satan or Lucifer who use to be in charge of God's praises.*

Now I ask you again with tears in my eyes (as I write this).

- Why isn't the Devil serving God?
- More importantly, why do people even listen to him?

The Devil is a liar, but **Jesus deserves our full attention to the glory of God the Father Amen**!

"GOD KEEPS HIS PROMISES"

One: God raised Jesus from the dead.
(Immortality/Eternity)

Two: God seated Jesus at his right side.
(Glory and honor)

Three: God made Jesus an heir in heaven.
(God prepared a place for him)

God has truly kept his word and promises. So we see, God is not a man, that he should lie or the son of man, that he should change his mind.*

"CHARACTER"

We should not lie to each other, but keep our word and not change our mind all the time (to be considered liars). A double minded man is unstable in all his or her ways, that person will not receive anything from the lord.*

The resurrection is really the hope we believe in because God raised Jesus from the dead and God is able to raise us also. (If we remain faithful until the end)*

There is nothing to hard for the lord. (God almighty)*

God truly loves his creation and God expects them to sincerely repent, when disciplined by God as children he delights in!*

"NO EXCUSES/MAKING A CHANGE"

Now we see (once again) that people are without excuse. God loves them. So ask yourself right now, (**Why don't people love God**?) They should!*

God is your best friend. God has promised never to leave you or forsake you and Jesus is a friend that sticks closer than a brother.*

Note: People leave God (they turn away from him).*

"REMEMBERING WHAT GOD HAS DONE"

Let us remember "Foot prints in the sand; during the roughest times of our life it was then, that God carried us through the storms of life."*

Please don't let go of Gods hand and don't give up!
(Let us walk with God as Jesus did)

"EXAMINING LOVE"

For someone to truly understand, **he or she must walk in love**. What is love?

(Good question) I thought you'd never ask because after all, the world gives you a different definition of love.

"WORLDLY LOVE"

The world says, I love you as long as you pay the bills, take me out to have fun, provide for me, pay the car note, groceries, trips, clothes and jewelry, but if you run out of money or material things; then I'm out of here, so long, see yah later, that's not love. It's a sad way to live.

(**That's spiritual death**) a life apart from God.

This is the reason the divorce rate is so high. People have made money there God.
(Especially in America)

Let's face it; America has become the (great whore) in the bible. America has the highest divorce rate among nations. American women are out of control with women's—lib. Women's—lib has under minded God's plan for perfect unity and union with God.*
America permits and promotes gay and lesbian marriages.

"WORLDLY LOVE"

America does not take care of its own citizens, but Americans are always in someone else's business.
(Country as well as individuals)

Americans are not busy at home, their busy playing games.
(Pleasure)

America continues to play God in politics with countries and people's lives.

The bible says: people listen to lies and they love it that way.
(False hood)*

America keeps picking (**electing**) false leaders who rob the country broke and lead them blindly into corruption.*

Jesus said; "All who came before me were **thieves and robbers**"*

"THIS IS LOVE"

(I think you get my point) Now this is love, not that we first loved God, but God first loved us and made a plan of salvation & redemption to draw us back to himself out of sin. God loved us even while we were still sinners.*

God is love because love comes from God. Whoever has been born again loves God and knows God.*

God's love is made complete in us, when we love one another.

We need not fear because the man who walks in love is made perfect by obeying God's command.*

"WALKING WITH GOD"

So we see that walking with God. The man of God is able to Learn from God and relies on God (by faith) because he truly knows that God loves him.*

Then the man of God is capable of teaching and instructing his wife then they (as a couple) can show their children (the right example) of how to live and please God.*

You cannot find this love, joy and peace in any other life style, but in (Holy marriage).

It trains people to be loving, kind, forgiving and able to work with one another for a common purpose (**to please God not themselves**).*

This creates unity and peace which transcend the true spirit of love. And this is love; to walk in obedience to God's commands or principles.

"OBEYING THE COMMAND OF LOVE"

As we obey Gods commands. We pass from death to life in God's presence. Since the darkness is passing, we see the love of God shining as a bright light that gives hope to all who see it.

(This is to the Father's glory)*

"REFUSING TO WALK IN LOVE"

What about the man who refuses to walk in love?
This person is a lost and restless soul that walks around in darkness because hate has blinded him.*

This person has been deceived by Satan because of his or her continual lust for the world (**to be friends with it**) in partnership with evil thoughts.*

This person's mind is unstable and reprobate because they can no longer distinguish good from evil. They hate because they do not know how to love and **the person must repent and turn to God** (Who is love).*

Why you ask?

Well let's break it down, the word of God tells us without love you can't gain anything as we seen earlier in the story of the vineyard. (Users)

So let us examine the characteristics of love very carefully and patiently.

- **To love or not to love, that is the question**?*

"THE MEANING OF LOVE"

The word of God tells us, that love is patient and kind, it does not envy or boast and it's not proud. It is not rude, self seeking or easily angered. It keeps no record of wrongs. Love does not delight in evil, but rejoices with the truth. It always protects, always trusts, always hopes and always perseveres. (Love never fails)*

This scripture tells us the very nature of God and the spirit of love. It tells us this divine nature is above worldly love.

One: Love tells us to go the extra mile with someone, especially our mate or spouse and children, but also with one another.*

Two: Love tells us the type of attitude, we should be displaying toward one another.*

Three: Love tells us not to be like the Devil, who was kicked out of heaven for being rude, proud and selfish with an at all cost mentally to get what he wanted.
(That's not love)*

Note: **I did not say what he needed**. The Devil was also easily angered.
(All borderlines of hatred)*

"THE MEANING OF LOVE"

Four: The scriptures tell us not to judge one another, not to keep a running inventory of wrongs, but to forgive sin. (One sin at a time)*

Five: Love tells us to be in agreement with the truth and not to be happy with someone's down fall. Love warns us to be aware of such an attitude, so we don't fall next.*

Six: Love tells us to help preserve people and encourage one another daily.*

Seven: Love tells us to endure hardship and walk as Jesus did. Love lets us know (**if we endure in it**) we will never fail in the sight of God and man!*

"WALKING IN LOVE"

So there you have it brothers and sisters of the lord (as long as we walk in love).
We need not fear, but rejoice in the true spirit of God.*

If we refuse to walk in love, then we can be sure the eyes of God are watching us in the light or the darkness.*
We should not be like unreasonable children and lean to our on understanding.

Because the scripture says: "When I was a child, I talked like a child, I reasoned like a child, but when I became a man. I put childish ways behind me. (A **man of God** that is)*

I understand now these three remain; Faith, Hope and love, but **the greatest of these is Love**!*

"BORN AGAIN/OVERCOMING"

So my friends, since God has shown us his great love. This love is found in the death, burial and resurrection of his son Jesus Christ.

A person must be born again to enter the kingdom of heaven or see it. Since we understand, then we are baptized into the Father, the Son and the Holy Spirit of love.
And the three are in agreement together.

Also: The water (baptism), the blood (of Jesus) and the Holy Spirit of (love and truth),
This testifies all are in agreement!

It lets us know the body will die, but **the spirit lives forever**!

"HOLY SPIRIT"

God has promised from the beginning to those who love him.*
(If they repent and are baptized)

They would receive the Holy Spirit. And this is how we know that he lives in us.

We know it by the spirit he (God) gave us.*
(The Spirit to Love)

Now let us walk in step with the spirit!

"THE GREATEST COMMANDS"

We see God has given us a set of commands to follow:
One: Love God with all your heart, soul, mind and strength. (First)*

Two: Love the family God gave you. (Spiritual home life)*

Three: And love your neighbors (God's creation)*

If we carry out God's commands, this will be love for God because his commands are not burdensome and everyone born of God overcomes the world.*

This will be our victory in God, even our faith to overcome the world by the blood of Jesus (forgiveness) and our testimony. (Holding to the truth in love)*

Since everything has been said, **simply believe it; like the faith of a little child trusting in his or her parents**.*

Do not add to it, do not take away from it or judgment will follow!

"CONCLUSION 2"

Now that God has shown us his great love. Know nothing in all creation should be able to separate us from the love of God that is in Christ Jesus. (**A higher form of love for God & people**)

Now read (Romans 8: 29-39) as a command.

Since God first loved you, also love God and this is truly the end of the matter!
(**Let no one deceive you**)

May the grace and peace of God guard your hearts Amen!

"THE MESSAGE"

Spirituality & A Stress Free Life Style: by Evangelist John Dye

The key to living a stress free life style is to understand Spirituality & Change; time does not stand still for anyone. If you refuse to change with the times, your letters in the mail will take 3 days to be delivered; instead of a few minutes by email. (Example: your life will take years to change, instead of a few days or months!)

My point is when you embrace Spirituality & Change, you will see changes starting to occur as God bring good things into your life; by faith you will make little changes daily/not by sight. Don't worry about what people think or say in time you will be a new person, but if you worry about what others think/by sight. It will take longer for you to change because some of these people in your life; have to be changed in order for you to move forward (This needs to happen, if you want to be content, stress free & happy with yourself & others!)

Example:

Religion is part of the problem because God never intended man to be religious, but spiritual. There are many who are traditionalized and destroying one another through envy, jealousy, discord & hatred, but there are others who are being born again in Spirit & Truth to love God and everyone else made in his image. (Humanity)

"THE MESSAGE"

In order for all people to live together in harmony, they must become spiritual people who walk by faith not by sight. Without Spirituality, there is no evidence of the fruits of the Spirit in most people's everyday life. (Their Religious, false or completely worldly)

The answer is: Everyone must become spiritual people, who walk by faith not by sight. So the fruits of the spirit; love, joy, peace, patience, goodness & righteousness can dwell in their hearts towards one another; then they will be able to Pray & Unite in Spirit & Truth for the Glory of God/not manmade religion. (Loving one another)

I like being a part of helping people achieve their dreams by giving them good advice! (Good Tips)

People talk, but the truth is religion does not work. Spirituality is the truth; people will have to embrace, if they want to change. (There is a difference) Religion is based on organizations that corrupt & take advantage of its members.

Spirituality is based on leading people to God to improve their individual lives, but people have to be re-trained to think spiritual/instead of being institutionalized by religion. That's why you see so many suffering people & scandals!

"THE MESSAGE"

Also: It's not always a good idea to confess to man, but you should always confess to God in your prayers! It's a good thing to make amends with yourself & reasonable people that except forgiveness & change.

I truly believe, we walk by faith & not by sight. It is when a person goes through something that greatness is discovered. Through losing a job, one becomes focused & creative to do that which he or she was created to do in the first place. By getting away from the crowd, you can realize your unique talents/instead of being manipulated by those around you on a daily basis who try to suppress your talents! (This will give you confidence in yourself because you're doing what you like & are good at. So pray to God, eat right, exercise & accomplish your goals then you will be happy & stress free)

People must have Faith, Proper Eating, Exercise and a Job they like; to meet their needs spiritually, physically, emotionally & socially. (Spirituality balances your life)

My mission is to improve the lives of people in this world, so they will love God & each other by motivating them to change from the pessimism of the world to optimism found in God for their own good. The results will be changes made in their Thinking & Life Style! (Successful Changes Bring Contentment)

"ABOUT THE AUTHOR"

Evangelist John Dye is an Author, Motivational Speaker and Spiritual Counselor that is constantly in touch with the needs of the people in accordance with God's will and grace. (As well as a Model/Actor & Athlete)

Also an Expert & Consultant on many issues that loves having deep discussion on air to help improve people's outlook toward each other from all walks & levels of life.

I have made a career out of helping people deal with life's issues. People, friends and family always turn to me in difficult times because they view my advice as the best you can get. I can answer all your questions because I'm very knowledgeable about every area of life!

Such as: News, Sports, Entertainment, Relationships, Spirituality and other topics. (Not tradition, but think outside the box)

www.heartministriesonline.com

God bless you!

"TESTIMONIES"

To Whom It May Concern:

I got saved March 28, 2004. As I began studying the Bible, I found it hard to understand, (KJV) Then I met John Dye and I was blessed by the way he explains the scriptures; he encouraged me to get a N.I.V study Bible, so I could have a better understanding on what I was reading.

Since we have started our Bible study in the mornings, John's wisdom has encouraged me to learn more and dig deeper into the pages of the Bible. John is the best preacher I have ever heard; he explains God's word so clear that I can understand it. John also has taught me not to worship earthly things in the flesh, but to worship our God in heaven in everything I do.

I believe God put John in here to teach, encourage and save some lives and I am one of them. John has been an inspiration to me and others, I believe he is a blessing sent from above to help us all see the light. Not only has John helped me to understand the Bible better, but he also helped me to understand my purpose in life! Thank you John!

Yours Truly, Josh Parkins

"TESTIMONIES"

To Whom It May Concern:

Thank you, John for sharing the word and giving me understanding of the Bible. John you are a good teacher and I love thanking you for the things in the Bible you taught me, God and his son Jesus is with you.

—I Corinthians 9:14
In the same way, the Lord has commanded that those who preach the gospel should receive their living from the Gospel.

God bless you!/Harold Sanders

To Whom It May Concern:

Brother Dye on your behalf, I write this letter in the highest regard. It has been a blessing to me as well as the whole ward for your humble presents. The Lord is with you and I pray all you do & say will prosper with holiness. It is a blessing from God for you being here teaching the broken hearted words of life, wisdom and peace. I thank you.

God bless you!/Tim Davis

"TESTIMONIES"

To Whom It May Concern:

My name is Marco R. Robinson; I would like to thank Brother Dye for coming into my life. He's showed & taught me so much about the Bible and the Heavenly Father up above. Even though my body is locked up, my mind is free. I'm at one of the happiest points of my life. I'm happy because I know my soul has been saved and I'm receiving the power to help save other lost souls. I would like to thank God for sending brother Dye into my life. May the good Lord bless brother Dye and his family the way He has blessed me!

Brother in the Lord, Marco Robinson

To Whom It May Concern:

I'm writing this letter in regards to Brother John Dye, I knew there was something very special about him; the way he talked and carried himself, his smile was bright and he always had a kind word for me. It brought a smile to my face to see him. He started a Bible study and I felt so lifted by the way he delivered the message. He's a real blessing to me. Thank You Brother Dye, wherever you may go, I know you'll take God's word with you!

Brother in Christ, Jeff Beatly

"TESTIMONIES"

To Whom It May Concern:

I prayed to the Lord and I asked for knowledge & wisdom.

Then I thanked the Lord for the gift because I had faith my prayer was already answered. We continued our prayers & fellowship and Brother Robinson was teaching me a lot. Then my prayer was answered, John Dye came to our dorm and we had Bible studies. And the way Brother John put the words he read, I knew right then that God sent him to teach me the knowledge and wisdom that I prayed for. I gave my life to the Lord around December 1, 2004 and I was baptized on January 9, 2005. I am proud that Brother John was there on that day to witness the occasion because God sent him to teach me. So for those of you who are reading this, John Dye is truly a man of God. He is wise and has a lot to offer to those who seek. He has worked wonders with me and he has taught me to understand the Bible. So friends pay very close attention to what this man has to say, God bless you all. John you are a blessing!!! Thank You!

Brother in Christ, Jim Powell

"TESTIMONIES"

To all the believers scattered abroad,

Greetings Saints, I have a few words that I would like to share with you. First, Prayer goes a long way in such perilous times. The prayer of a righteous man avails much. My brethren, Jesus said to know the day & hour of your visitation. Jesus wept over Jerusalem before he entered therein because they knew not, their day of visitation. He came unto his own and they received him not.

I met a strong Brother in Lord, who has been a very present help in a time of desperation & desolation and by the Word of God he brought in restoration. My Brethren, these words aren't for everyone, but to whom they are given. (Isaiah 53 says, "Who has believed thy message") Brother Dye has brought a word & not only a word, but the Living Word to those bound in sin. (Isaiah 61 says, "The Spirit of the Lord is upon me; because the Lord hath anointed me to preach the gospel unto the meek. He hath proclaimed liberty to the captives & brokenhearted; also the opening of the prison to those who are bound.") I must say, since we have received Brother Dye, the chain of bondage has been broken by the Holy Spirit, because the Word says, where the Spirit of God is there's Liberty. My brethren, I testify & encourage you to receive Brother Dye as one of God's elect. He's been a faith ambassador for God and he loves Him and His flock. I wanted to express to the congregation, that I am grateful for meeting him and I hope you are as well.

Brother in Christ, Chaz Jackson

"TESTIMONIES"

To Whom It May Concern:

I thank Brother John Dye, for his words and wisdom about our Heavenly Father & Jesus. Brother Dye has given me a better understanding of the Lord and the word of the Lord. Brother Dye is a blessing of God. He has given me something more to look forward to as my life goes on in this world. When times are a little hard for me, I asked Brother Dye for advice, words of wisdom and prayer; that everything will be okay. I praise Brother Dye and give him thanks for being here and for helping those who want to hear the word of the Lord. So they too, can lead a more spiritual life/so, in all who thank him for his blessing. I say, "Praise Brother Dye and thank him for all he has done." "In Jesus name" Amen.

Matthew L. Luthringer

To Whom It May Concern:

Brother John Dye! May you be blessed in life because you have been a true blessing to us all in ward #5. You have given us all a peace of mind and have encouraged us all to live the word of God. You've made a difference in our lives and the way we see it.

God sent us an angel and that's you my Brother. I would like to hear the word more from you on the street. My information will be with this. May God bless you and yours always!

Your brother, Drake Newton

"GODS IN CONTROL"

If you examine the recent events in society then you will be able to see God is in control and he's removing people from power & authority because of abuse & corruption. You see many priests being removed & prosecuted for abusing some children & members of their church congregation. (It's sad because some of the children were deaf and they could not speak for themselves, but were taken advantage of by their overseers) People have died in sweat lodges because of preachers & overseers tricking them with gimmicks to get their money. Many preachers are stepping down because their announcing they're gay or lesbian like the book of Romans tells us. Senators, CEOs, Banking Officials, College Professor's and School Teachers are resigning or being fired for financial abuse, scandals and taking advantage of their members; as was written in Timothy Chapter 3.

(Also great Natural Disasters & Weather in unexpected places)

My friends don't be deceived, God cannot be mocked and he sent me to deliver this message to you; like Isaiah Chapter 53(Pay attention to what I'm saying, so many of you will be saved) My every word has come to pass, read my books, watch my DVDs and listen to my CDs & Interviews because they foretold everything before it happen. Let them who have an ear/hear the truth. The Bible says, if a man comes and his words come to pass then know, he is from God and this is your day of visitation to be healed & saved. **God bless you all.**

"INTERVIEW OF ME & LIFE"

Ev. John Dye**:** www.troyceo.com March Magazine 106-110

Who is John Dye as a kid?

I was a smart and athletic individual that was competitive in everything I did from sports to life (on or off the court or field) in or out of school my mind was set on overcoming all obstacle set before me. I was a self taught person that was good at everything; I put my mind or hands too. I could sing & dance, play basketball, & football or gymnastics and I never let people's opinion or jealousy stop me from excelling in what I was doing. People in the real world saw, I had true God given talent, but schools, organizations and the system were more political in nature. The best people were not being exalted and that taught me something about life. (I was a winner, an over-comer)

What made you get so involved with the Lord and church?

I did not grow up in church, but I knew I was from God because I could feel the presence of God around me all the time. People use to call me the philosopher because I was always explaining things. (In 1995 God visited me and talked with me about my mission)

I started helping people in every area of life and from all walks of life. I handed out many Bibles & gave many Bible studies; encouraging people to turn back to God before it was too late because I saw God was being removed from every area of life.

"INTERVIEW OF ME & LIFE"

People who owed institutions weeded God out of schools, politics, finances, corporations, social functions & religions; although there were a lot of churches, the people in those churches were more ungodly than some who never attended. The manipulation was so strong in these institutions; people were allowing themselves to be taken advantage of because they were blinded by the number of people who attended. (That type of ignorance does not come from God)

They weeded God out first, so they could take advantage of the people because they knew the people wouldn't have any self-esteem or common sense left. (To peacefully protest)

What does a spiritual counselor do?

A Spiritual Counselor's job is to make the people of a generation aware that God is being replaced in the society with other things and it will cause their down fall.

My job as the man of God is to make you aware of this fact and lead you to the glory of God. So God can lead you to a blessing and bring you home in glory.

The messenger is spiritual & not religious (He is loyal & dedicated to God almighty and no other) He can't be bought or persuaded not to deliver Gods message.

"INTERVIEW OF ME & LIFE"

What is Heart Ministries?

Heart Ministries is the truth because God is something that happens in the heart of people/not from an outward opinion. It's when you know your life is going to change & never be the same again because God is in control & no one can stop it, but it's good for you!

Heart Ministries Online.com is the vision God gave me to reach the people in the world, deliver his message and let them know; the man of God is in the world during their life time! (So they can contact him & support him in this mission)

My mission is to improve the lives of people in this world, so they will love God & each other by motivating them to change from the pessimism of the world to optimism found in God for their own good. The results will be changes made in their Thinking & Life Style! (Successful Changes Bring Contentment) http://www.heartministriesonline.com/book.html,

"INTERVIEW OF ME & LIFE"

Heart Ministries Prevention Program (HMPP), provides people and their loved ones with counseling for: parenting, relationship issues, substance abuse, violence, gang, release from prison issues, stress and emotional difficulties pertaining to life as well as Spiritual help geared toward making their life better!

Contact me through the web form, email or call, then an appointment will be set up that will greatly increase your life and situation.

Evangelist John Dye is addressing all the issues people are dealing with now!

So get involved & stay connected by Sponsoring, Donating or telling someone you know for their good. God bless you,

Contact Evangelist John Dye **(Your support will help people)**
www.heartminisriesonline.com

"INTERVIEW OF ME & LIFE"

What is your take on churches today and the mega church?

The churches today are institutions like corporations; they should not be viewed as instruments of God because they are manipulating those in the buildings. The building is not the church, the people are the church and they should listen to God and make the world a better place for all people; instead of promoting a religion. Religion doesn't work because it focuses on the outward appearance & buildings, but spirituality understands people will change in Gods time anywhere. (The inward change of the heart & soul)

God never intended people to be religious or worship in buildings, God expects you to worship in spirit & truth everywhere and love one another!

"INTERVIEW OF ME & LIFE"

What about the Youth and Proper parenting?

The Country is so far from God that the parents never learned proper parenting. They break spiritual laws to become friends with their children and that caused their children to lose respect for them.

God teaches you to keep the parent child relationship in place, so you can help the child through the manipulation & trouble of world. God doesn't want parents helping children destroy themselves by participating & manipulating them. Parent should try to encourage children to do what's right, praise God and love all people. (So they will be well rounded individuals)

"INTERVIEW OF ME & LIFE"

As a black man, I have been spanked before and feel I am better for it. What is your take on spanking?

I have DVDs on many topics that are outstanding teaching material.

I believe you should spank children while their little to show them right from wrong to establish the parent child relationship and boundaries of the house. I believe this will raise them to be respectful & responsible people in the world.

I don't believe in forcing children as they get older or anyone to do things that are not good or against they're will. There are systems in place for hard headed people who refuse to do what's right.

The Bible says: disobedient children are cut off, spare the rod & spoil the child and the way of the transgressor is hard. An occasional spanking does not hurt the child.

"INTERVIEW OF ME & LIFE"

Okay, now sports. What is your take on the pro football lockout?

The fans don't need to go through a lock out because the owners won't open their books. So they should give the players union what it ask for. It's simple; there can't be fair negotiations with owners who won't open their books for accountability.

Do you feel there should be any changes in the NFL?

Yes, The NFL's ruining the game (It's not flag football) this is what happens when you have too many rules. We all know there are injuries that come with contact sports like football & boxing, but you have to implement fines based on individuals doing dirty things to intentionally hurt people; like in boxing; biting someone's ear or head butting that's obvious, in football; spearing someone with your head first intentionally or under cutting people to hurt their legs.

"INTERVIEW OF ME & LIFE"

The NFL should review plays and fine the team for dirty play. So the behavior is not taught as a team concept. Also I hate stripping the ball from players while standing them up. (I like the days when you had to tackle people and if the ball came loose during a tackle that was a fumble) NFL teams now are poor tacklers because of this stripping and it's ruining the future & integrity of the game!

The NFL should let the players express themselves when scoring touch downs because that's part of the human spirit of accomplishment to celebrate your success in your unique way. (Stop oppressing and depressing the players, fans & game)

What about the 18 game season?

I don't like the longer season because I like comparing what other athletes did in their generation with the same amount of games. Like Kobe Bryant on paper, maybe a better basketball player in his generation than Michael Jordan because of his accomplishments being completed earlier, but we all know Michael Jordan had a competitive drive & incredible will to win, like no other in basketball and that makes him the best!

"INTERVIEW OF ME & LIFE"

A quick baseball question if you follow. The future of the Yankees; what's your feeling?

The Yankees will always be competitive because they put money behind their team & players, but the other teams have caught up talent wise and money can't change that fact.
(Like the NBA, one star want do it anymore; you need 3 or more good players.)

What is your take on blacks in black history only represented in one month?

That's what wrong with America; it down plays the accomplishments & contributions of minorities and others in the nation & world. Also it teaches lies to children by replacing truth with myths in school books then when they grow up; they learn the truth.

"INTERVIEW OF ME & LIFE"

Blacks have done outstanding things in society and with great character, despite all they have been put through by this country. They should be celebrated all year long and in school books, so the children will know the truth from the start.

Look at all the criticism President Barak Obama went through about his name, color, faith and ability to lead the Country, but they continue to over look his accomplishments. If they can do this to a half black man at the top of society; what do you think is happening to the black people & minorities throughout the society including the poor?

"INTERVIEW OF ME & LIFE"

What about today's culture, do you see it as pop culture? I ask this because the slang and style of all, seems to have an urban feel. For example saying: That's Wassup, Swagga, Pants hanging down or being gangster

The world is changing all around us rapidly and those who change with the times will benefit from the changes being made. (Love, peace, equality & justice)
Not all the changes are good, but that's part of growing pains.

Freedom of expression in music, culture, fashion, religion and politics is Spiritualities way of balancing out life. The internet & technology lets us know what's going on in our society; so we can make adjustments to our societies for the better. Slang, texting, email and blogs, allow people to talk all around the world to stop corruption and promote individuality for better or worse, but common sense should be used while interacting.

"INTERVIEW OF ME & LIFE"

What is your feeling on the bullying going on today?

Once again the apple doesn't fall to far from the tree, some of the children are picking up their parents ways; where bulling is being taught by family members.
Others are just mean children, crying out for the wrong kind of attention; they need help because the loving characteristics that come from knowing God is missing in their life & society.

This is what Jesus was trying to tell the people of his generation. (Rome was very violent) The same thing Martin Luther King Jr. tried to tell America in his generation. I'm telling you they all need God, the parents & children to stop the violence that's harming the children and people today.

"INTERVIEW OF ME & LIFE"

Anything you would like to add?

Evangelist John Dye's Wisdom, Book, DVDs & CDs are changing the world. (You must read & see for yourself/to embrace the truth; he brings to light)

John Dye's other achievements Include: A Modeling & Acting career that has featured him in Commercials, Photo Shoots, Films and TV Series such as: **The Beast** w/Patrick Swayze, **ER** w/Mekhi Phifer, **Baby on Board** w/Jerry O'Connell, **Nothing like the Holidays** w/John Leguizamo & **Contagion** w/Laurence Fishburne. (**Roles:** FBI Agent, Fireman, Military, Court room, Dance, Ballroom & Park Scenes)

See my photo profile on http://www.nextcat.com/johndye

Real Talent Inc. Modeling Agency/Chicago: http://www.realtalentinc.com/

When you want it done right call **Multi-talented John Dye**/He is a great **Public Speaker!**

Contact Evangelist John Dye: 574-220-3363/Author, Actor, Model, Athlete, Consultant, Life Coach, Spokes Person & Motivational Speaker http://www.heartminisriesonline.com

"UNITED NATIONS"

To: Ban Ki-Moon/UN Secretary General

Hello, my name is Evangelist John Dye and I have a message for the world and its leaders. (Whether they are Presidents, Kings, Queens, Diplomats, Ambassadors, Cabinet members or any other name they chose to call themselves these days.)

It's time for them to take a step back from power and reflect on the world they live in to see, if they are part of the problem or part of the solution in Gods sight.

It is time to look at the big picture in order to save the world; we live in. We only have one world and it's up to mankind to take care of it. Because of a few people in high places not understanding the spiritual implications of the positions they hold and the effect it has on the world and humanity. Satan has run his course destroying the hearts, minds & souls of the people in the biggest cities to smallest villages and it all started at the top.

I was sent, so you would understand the truth.

(Blessed is he, who comes in the name of the Lord)

"UNITED NATIONS"

Let me explain, you leaders have tasted the good of the land in every way: economically (financial), physically (pleasures), mentally (demanding), emotionally (joyful) and this all came at the expense of the oppression placed on the less fortunate in your societies. You have made yourselves rich through selfishness. Your selfish indulgence and carelessness for average people in life has blinded you to the big picture. The truth about humanity and Gods will on Earth for life.

Now we find ourselves in the darkest times of our lives because capitalism rules the day, through gold, diamonds, jewels, wire transfers and the love of money. (That's why the economy failed because people were taught to believe in money over God)

It's so sad, that the love of many have grown cold.

With so many hearts, minds and souls crushed at the expense of a few people in high places. It's no surprise that people are doing anything they can to survive and violence & crime are high because they've been neglected of their basic needs in life. (You have to give them hope of a better future!)

"UNITED NATIONS"

Since the fall of the economy, the rich are starting to see; how the poor feels and the shoes are being put on the other side's feet.

The leaders know that the average people have not had the opportunity for life, liberty and the pursuit of happiness in any Country.

It is time that we set all of our differences aside to bring love and humanity back to the world for the glory of God. I urge every man, woman and child to pray earnestly for this spiritual global mission.

If man can turn a desert into a city like Las Vegas with modern technology; then you should be able to feed, clothe and supply the basic needs of people & put a smile on the faces of those in the remotest part of the world. You can do it!

If man can build "Atom & Nuclear Bombs" to destroy the world then let us come together and do something great to lift up the hearts, minds, health and souls of the individuals in this world. God has commanded us to do it.

Let us love one another. (You must change to save the world)

By Evangelist John Dye/www.heartministriesonline.com

"NEW HELPER PROGRAM"

I would like to speak with you about my new program: Call Immediately.

#1

Changing your life:

My program is changing the lives of people.

If you want help for yourself then you need this program.

You cannot afford to wait any longer, now is the time for you to change.

I'm dedicated to helping you change your life at this moment in time.

#2

Making a Difference: Member Help Services Program

Members have the ability to help make a difference in the lives of others by giving to the Spiritual leader of your time to help him spread the message of God in the lives of others for their good and well being.

"NEW HELPER PROGRAM"

It means you understand the principle of giving and receiving, everyone on these lists will help others & the Ministry which is their duty to God and receive a gift periodically when their name comes up in the rotation cycle. You will also be made aware of future Seminars & Meetings!
(**Please give, what you can afford**)

Members Giving: Above & Beyond-unlimited amount,

Weekly

Bi-weekly

Monthly

2Cor. 9:7 (Each man should give what he has decided in his heart to give, not reluctantly or under compulsion, for God loves a cheerful giver.)

Please send Donations to **Evangelist John Dye**:
Heart Ministries Online
P.O. Box 722
Mishawaka, IN. 46546

Thank God,

Evangelist John Dye/574-220-3363/
www.heartministriesonline.com

"THANKS FOR YOUR SUPPORT"

Heart Ministries Online.com "Supporters"

I want to thank you for supporting:
Heart Ministries Online & Evangelist John Dye

I really appreciate your support in helping me get the *"Truth"* out in many forms such as: Books, DVDs, CDs and Speaking.

I want you to know your contribution has not been in vain, but it has gone toward changing the hearts, minds and souls of the people in this world.

Bringing them to an understanding of: (The Way, Truth and Life) God predestined for us before time began (through Love)!

Thank you, once again for your support.

"CONTRIBUTIONS"

If you wish to send future contributions/send support to:

Heart Ministries Online.com
Attn: Evangelist: John Dye
P.O. Box 722
Mishawaka, Indiana 46546
Cell: (574) 220-3363

Supporters:
Assistant Minister: Terry (of Goshen)

Sincerely,

Evangelist John Dye
www.heartministriesonline.com

"VOICE OF PEOPLE"

To: Whom it may concern
From: Voice of the People
(These are a combination of sayings from many people, I met)

We are writing because we have encountered an extraordinary individual on this planet in America. His name is Evangelist John Dye (man of God) we have never met anyone who lives up to the name like this man sent by God.

This man has touched, helped & healed the hearts and minds of so many people. You must meet him for yourself and then you will know he is not from this world and that's a good thing. (The Spirit of the Lord rest on him in a mighty way)
He is truly anointed.

He is a person that you can sense love flow from him to you. You can tell he is genuinely concerned about your affairs or problems and he is willing to help. (Not only help, but has the answer to all your questions about life)

"VOICE OF THE PEOPLE"

Wise is an understatement to make about "Dr, Rev, Teacher, Minister, Counselor: Evangelist John Dye (man of God)." He is so much more; **a friend that sticks closer than a brother**"

We have prayed and he has come our way to answer our prayers as well as fulfill the prayers of so many others. Thank God for sending him into our lives and this world. We need him more than ever in these terrible times.

So please allow this man to speak, so he can teach and reach the world. He's someone who has been in the spiritual, mental, emotional and physical battle fighting for Gods people to deliver them from evil.

There is no doubt in our mind, that this man deserves the" Noble peace prize" for all the hard work and lives he has touched for God!

We think you should do a major story on him during these false and terrible times because he speaks the truth! He should meet all the "Leaders in this Country and the World." We believe this would be in every body's best interest to bring Truth and Peace to the world because (**John is sent by God**).

He can use all the supporters that he can get to help him do the good. (**God has called him to do**)!

Thank you, voice of the people!

"DID THIS BOOK HELP YOU"

If so please send your replies & testimonies to:
Heart Ministries Online P.O. Box 722, Mishawaka, IN 46546
Attn: Evangelist John Dye
Please mail, call or log-on www.heartministriesonline.com

Heart Ministries Online DVDs & CDs

1. Why worry.
2. God's way is higher.
3. Don't let sin keep you from God.
4. What's a famine?
5. Love with action and deeds not words.
6. Raising the standard.
7. Be careful what you listen too.
8. The truth will set you free.
9. Everybody has a chance.
10. If you care
11. God is first not last
12. Suffering for good
13. Be sure
14. Blessings and Curses
15. There is one who knew
16. Opposites attract
17. Spiritual Warfare
18. A Tree and its Fruit
19. The Lord's Prayer
20. The End
21. Our Times
22. A Personal Relationship with God

"BIOGRAPHY"

(I knew, I was from God as a little child)
I was born in Gary, Indiana. My mother's name was Mary and she was from down south or (southern part of the United States). I never had a Dad; (God) is the only father, I ever knew. My mother moved me away from Gary, IN. as a baby to Elkhart, IN.
I would talk about God to my siblings and mother as a child growing up in our home and then I moved with my uncle around the age of twelve. (Enjoying sports)

While in Elkhart, I attended Hawthorne Elementary and Pierre Moran Jr. High at these Schools, I won numerous Championships from fifth to the ninth grade in Football, Basketball and Track. I went on to Central High School where I played in every Sectional Championship Basketball game for three years. The point is God was establishing me as a winner and leader from the very beginning.

I was good at everything, I put my hands too.
I attended Marian College in Indianapolis, IN. briefly for Basketball, but certain events brought me back to Elkhart. Then I realized the role Politics played in people's lives and how unfair or prejudice people could be toward each other.

"BIOGRAPHY"

Elkhart showed me the lowest level of life in every way imaginable morally, mentally, physically and spiritually. The quality of people's lives was not good and the way they treated one another was even worse. The prejudice attitude was at an all time high (especially in work places) as well as social functions. You could see the division!

I observed selfishness and ignorance at its best through poverty, drug abuse and alcoholism. Also hatred, discord and jealousy played major roles in people's destruction. It all stemmed from an economy that was divided. God showed all this to me (as he shaped and molded me) so that I would be able to save his people in the future.

In 1995 God appeared to me and talked with me to tell me my mission. God filled me with his spirit, wisdom, truth, love and understanding (above all things).

I am the man of God. Since then, God has up held my every word.

God Bless You,

Evangelist John Dye

"SCRIPTURE INDEX 1"

Scriptures are in order from beginning to end of book for study.

Walking with God/Scripture Indexes 1

Mt 18:4
Gen 1:27
Pr 22:6
Isa 1:18
Job 1:12
Eph 6:11
Mt 4:1-11
2Pe 2:18
1Cor 7:5
Heb 2:1-5
Heb 10:8-18
Gen 28:10-22
Lk 10:24
Ne 9:26
Isa 55:6-9
Rev 4:11
Ro 3:23
1Pe 3:15
Zech 3:1-2
Ro 13:12
1Pe 1:4
2Tim 2:25-26
1Cor 10:13
Heb 3:12-13
Gen 28:12
Jn. 1:51
Lk 11:48-49
Lk 24:25-44

"SCRIPTURE INDEX 1"

Ac 3: 24

2Ch 35:18

Mt 23:37

2Pe 3

Ac 2:21

Joel 2:32

Eccl 6:5

Ps 51:13

Ro 14:13

Joel 3:14

Dan 10: 11-12

Lk 16:19-31

Jn 8:31-47

Heb 6:4-12

Eccl 5:10

1Tim 6:6

Ro 11:3

1Ki 19

2Pe 1

Eccl 9:12

Ro 10:13

Ac 5:1-13

Pr 14:12

Ezek. 7:19

Ro 3:23

Pr 11:28

Nu 12

Mt 10:28

Mt 18:6

1Jn 2:15-17

Isa 56:11

Rev 4:8

"SCRIPTURE INDEX 1"

"SCRIPTURE INDEX 1"

"SCRIPTURE INDEX 1"

"SCRIPTURE INDEX 1"

"SCRIPTURE INDEX 1"

1Jn 2:8-11

1Jn 5:21

2Jn 2:6

1sa 16:6-8

1Tim 4:18

Pr 18:16

Ro 7:19-21

1Cor 13:12

Ac 3:1-3

Dt. 4:7

Dt. 10:17

Mt 6:33

1Tim 6:6

Heb 2

2Ch 16:9

Rev 2:7

Dt. 8

2Cor 5:7

Ac 20:35

2Cor 9:7

1Cor 9:14

Lk. 6:38

Heb 3:12-19

1Cor 8:1-3

Dt. 3:24

Heb 11:6

Gen 3

Php 4:12

Heb 4

Job 1:20

"SCRIPTURE INDEX 1"

"SCRIPTURE INDEX 2"

And This Is Love/Scripture Indexes 2

Ex 19: 5-6	Lk. 6: 39-40		
Dt. 4: 1-40	Gen. 2: 7		
Dt. 6: 1-25	Gen. 2: 19		
1Cor. 2: 6-16	Gen. 2: 18-24,		
1Cor. 7: 15-20	1Cor. 7: 39	Gen. 2: 24,	
1Cor. 9: 5-6	1Tim. 3: 1-15,		
1Cor. 11: 7-12	Gen. 3: 17,		
1Cor. 13: 1-13	1Tim. 2: 11-15,		
1Pe. 3: 1-22	Eph. 6: 1-4,		
2Pe. 1: 3-4	Col. 3: 20,		
2Pe. 1: 19-21	1Tim. 4: 1-16,		
1Tim 2: 1-15	2Tim 3: 16-17,		
Lev. 19: 1-4	Tit. 2: 1-15,		
Mt. 28: 18-20	Heb. 5 11-14,		
Ex. 19: 3-8	Heb. 12: 7-15	Job 1: 6	
Ex. 31: 12-13	Gen. 2: 1-3	Dt. 30: 19-20	
Jn. 3: 1-21	Rev. Ch. 12	Rev. 12: 12	
Jn. 4: 23-24	Rev. 12: 7-8	2Cor. 11: 14	
Act. 2: 40-41	Dan. 8: 15-19	Rev. 12: 9	
Eph. 1; 5, 11	Isa. 14: 12-23	2Cor. 2: 11	
Ac. 2: 39	Rev. 12: 3-4, 7-9	Eph. 6: 10-12	
Mt. 12: 48-50	Jude 9	Gen. 3: 1	
Gen. 1: 1-8	Dan. 10: 13, 21	Mt. 4: 1-11	
Gen. 12: 1-3	Dan. 12: 1	Gen. 3: 2-3	Gen. 2: 1-3
Dan. 9: 20-23	Hab. 2: 2-4		

"SCRIPTURE INDEX 2"

Gen. 1:31	Lk 1: 11-20	1Cor. 10: 1-13	
Gen. 13: 14-18	Lk. 1: 26-38	Ps. 1: 3	
Gen. 26: 2-6	Job 1: 6	Eph. 5: 22-28	
Gen. 28: 10-14	Zech. 3: 2	1Cor. 11: 1-3	
Ac. 3: 17-26	Mt. 16: 23	Ps. 1: 3	
Ac. 17: 24-34	Pr. 15: 3	2Cor. 10: 3-8	
Ro. 4: 16-25	Rev. 12: 3,4,7,9	1Cor. 8: 1	
Eccl. 4: 12	Rev. 12: 7-9	Ge.3: 6	
Mt. 19: 4-6	Mk. 4: 15	Gen. 39: 6-12	
Gen. 3: 9-13, 17	2Cor. 11: 14	Gen. 3: 17	
Gen. 2: 4-8	Rev. 12: 9	1Ki. 11: 1-4, 7-9	
Gen. 2: 16-17	Rev. 20: 2, 7	Eph. 5: 22-24	
Gen. 15: 1	Dt. 17: 2-5	Pr. 31: 1-3	
Pr. 22: 6	Dt. 17: 6-7	1Pe. 3: 7	
Gen. 1: 28	Dt. 17: 2-4	1Tim. 2: 14	
Phil. 4: 12	Rev. 12: 12	2 Cor. 11: 3	
Heb. 11: 1	Rev. 12: 7-9, 12	Rev 12: 17	Gen. 3: 11-13
1Cor. 9: 24-27	Isa. 14: 12-23		
Jer. 5: 1-3	Gen. 17: 1-14	2Tim. 3: 1-5	Jer. 9: 3-9
Heb. 4: 13	2Tim. 3: 16		
Jer. 6: 10	Gen. 3: 9		

"SCRIPTURE INDEX 2"

"SCRIPTURE INDEX 2"

Ps. 54: 7
Ac. 2: 21
Joel 2: 32
Ro. 10: 13
Isa. 53: 1
2Cor. 2: 14-17
2Cor. 2: 6-11
2Cor. 7: 8-13
Ac. 2: 39-41
2Cor. 7:1
Gen. 3: 17
Gen. 3: 13
Gen. 3: 16
Gen. 3: 15
Eph. 6: 12
Rev. 12: 4-7
2Cor. 6: 16-17
1Jn. 2: 15-17
2Cor. 6: 14-18
Phil. 4: 4-9
2 Pe.2: 4-10
2Pe. 2: 7-8
Gen. 39: 8-10
Jdg. 16: 16
1Jn. 4: 5-6
Pr. 3: 5-6
Gen. 39: 7-10
1Jn. 1: 9
Ps. 47: 8
Rev. 3: 21
Rev. 22: 1-6
Lk. 5: 31-32
Lk. 24: 44-47
Ac. 1: 4-8
Lk. 24: 48-49
Jn. 4: 21-24
1Tim. 5: 14-15
1Tim. 6: 17-21
Ps. 11: 4
Isa. 6: 1
Heb. 1: 1-14
2Pe. 1: 21
Heb. 2: 4
2Th. 2: 13
Phil. 2: 1-9
2Tim. 1: 12-14
Ro. 8: 1-27
2Cor. 1: 2-11
2Tim. 2: 14-26
2Tim. 4: 16
1Th. 1: 5
Jn. 16: 1-16
Jn. 15: 26
Jn. 14: 15-31
Lk.24: 47
Ac. 20-21
Ac. 26: 20
Ro. 2: 4
2Pe. 3-9
Jn. 16: 26-27
Mt. 21: 33-41
Lk. 9: 25
1Cor. 10: 6-11
2Ki. 1: 1-10
2Cor. 2: 11
Eph. 6: 11
Jn. 3: 6
Jn. 3: 21
Jn. 3: 19-20
Jn. 15: 25
Eph. 5: 11
1Jn. 3: 4-12
Isa. 53:1
2Ki. 20: 1-7
Jn. 14: 12
1Jn. 4: 10
Heb. 12:1-8
2Tim. 3:-12
Jn. 21: 15-17
2Cor. 5: 20-21
Ez. Ch. 34

"SCRIPTURE INDEX 2"

1Tim. 3: 12-13
Gen. 2: 24
1Cor. 6: 12-20
1Cor. 9: 24-27
Gen. 39: 6
Phil. 4: 8
1Tim. 4: 8
2Tim. 2: 3-12
1Cor. 4: 12
Rev. 12: 10-11
Mt. 10: 22-28
Mt. 24: 9-14
Heb. 2: 5-11
Heb. 12: 2
1Pe. 3: 21-22
Heb. 2: 3-11
Jas. 1: 17-18
Isa. 14: 12
Nu. 23: 19
Jas. 1: 5-8
Heb. 2: 11-18
Gen. 18: 13-15
Lk. 24: 44-48
Heb. 12: 5-8
Heb. 8: 7-13
Heb. 10: 5-18
Jn. 6: 44-45
Heb. 2: 4
1Sa. 16:12
2Ch. 7: 14-22
Jonah 1: 1-3
1Cor. 13: 4-8
Mt. 5: 40-42
1Jn. 3: 11-24
Isa. 14: 12
Rev. 12: 7-9
Gal. 5: 19-20
Mt. 7: 1-5
Gal. 6: 7-9
Mt. 7: 1-5
Gal. 6: 7-9
Gal. 6: 1, 10
2Pe. 1: 3-11
1Jn. 4: 18
1Pe. 3: 12
1Cor. 13: 11
1Cor. 13: 13
Jn. 3: 16
Heb. 4: 12
2Tim. 3:16-17
Lk. 11: 39-54
Heb. 11: 1-40
Jas. 4: 7-8
1Jn. 4: 10
Heb. 12: 1-8
Jn. 14: 12

"SCRIPTURE INDEX 2"

Ro. 1: 20
Dt. 31: 6
Heb. 13: 5
Pr. 18: 24
Heb. 3: 12
Job 42: 10-16
1Jn. 2: 5-6
1Tim 2: 11-14
1Tim. 3: 11
1Tim. 5: 13-15
Tit. 2: 3-5
Jn. 8: 42-47
Tit. 1: 10-16
Mt. 15: 14
Ac. 2: 40
1Cor. 15: 33-34
1Jn. 4: 10, 19
1Jn. 4: 7-8
1Jn. 4: 16-18
1Jn. 4: 16
Eph. 5: 22-28
1Cor. 14: 35
Gal. 5: 22-23
2Jn. 1: 6
1Jn. 3: 14
1Jn. 4: 20
1Jn. 2: 15-17
Lk. 24: 45-48
1Cor. 15: 20-28
Jn. 3: 3-7
Mt. 28: 5-10, 16-20
1Jn. 5: 6-8
1Cor. 2: 6-16
1Jn. 3: 24
Mk. 12: 29-30
Mt. 13: 48-50
Gal. 6: 10
Mk 12: 31
1Jn. 5: 1-3
1Jn. 5: 4-5
Jn. 16: 33
Jn. 16: 33
Mt. 18: 1-3
Rev. 22: 18-21
Ro. 1: 18-32
1Tim 4: 1-5
1Cor. 13: 1-3

CPSIA information can be obtained at www.ICGtesting.com
Printed in the USA
BVOW031851060213

312596BV00003B/188/P